Michael Hastings was born in 1938, and brought up in Brixton where he still lives. At fifteen he commenced a three-year apprenticeship in bespoke tailoring. He has written five novels – *The Game* (1957), *The Frauds* (1959), *Tussy is Me* (1968), *The Nightcomers* (1971) and *And in the Forest the Indians* (1975); a collection of short stories, *Bart's Mornings and Other Tales of Modern Brazil* (1975); and two biographies, *Rupert Brooke: 'The Handsomest Young Man in England'* (1969) and *Sir Richard Burton* (1978).

His plays are: *Don't Destroy Me*, directed by Robert Peake, 1956; *Yes and After*, directed by John Dexter, 1957; *The World's Baby*, directed by Patrick Dromgoole, 1964; *For the West (Congo)*, directed by Toby Robertson, 1965; *Blue as His Eyes the Tin Helmet He Wore*, directed by David Cunliffe, 1966; *Lee Harvey Oswald: 'a far mean streak of indepence brought on by negleck'*, directed by Peter Coe, 1967; *The Silence of Saint-Just*, directed by Walter Eyselink, 1972; *The Cutting of the Cloth*, unperformed autobiographic play, 1973; *For the West (Uganda)*, directed by Nicholas Wright, 1977; *Gloo Joo*, directed by Michael Rudman, 1978; *Full Frontal*, directed by Rufus Collins, 1979; *Carnival War*, directed by Antonia Bird, 1979; *Gloo Joo*, TV, directed by John Kaye Cooper, 1979; *Murder Rap*, TV, directed by Peter Duffell, 1980; *Midnight at the Starlight*, directed for Yorkshire Television by John Glenister, 1980, and *Midnite at the Starlite*, directed by Bill Pryde, 1981, for the Birmingham Studio Theatre.

Michael Hastings has won several awards, including the Academy of Arts and Sciences 'Emmy', the Somerset Maugham Award, the *Evening Standard* Comedy of the Year, BAFTA and Writers' Guild awards. He was the subject of a programme in the BBC's *Writers and Places* series, entitled *Michael Hastings in Brixton*, TV, directed by Sandra Gregory, 1980.

MICHAEL HASTINGS

Carnival War
Midnite at the Starlite

PENGUIN BOOKS

Penguin Books Ltd, Harmondsworth, Middlesex, England
Penguin Books, 625 Madison Avenue, New York, New York 10022, U.S.A.
Penguin Books Australia Ltd, Ringwood, Victoria, Australia
Penguin Books Canada Ltd, 2801 John Street, Markham, Ontario, Canada L3R 1B4
Penguin Books (N.Z.) Ltd, 182–190 Wairau Road, Auckland 10, New Zealand

Published in Penguin Books 1981

The song 'Sailing' which appears on page 69 was written by Gavin Sutherland,
© 1972 Island Music Ltd. 22 St Peter's Square, London W6, England.

Typeset, printed and bound in Great Britain by
Hazell Watson & Viney Ltd, Aylesbury, Bucks
Set in Monotype Imprint

CONTENTS

Carnival War

Carnival War was first performed at the Theatre Upstairs, Royal Court Theatre, London, on 15 August 1979 with the following cast:

Driss	BERNARD GALLAGHER
Raine	SUE LYNNE
Beverley	KATE SAUNDERS
Alice	CLAIRE WALKER
Firestone	BURT CAESAR
Doug	HAROLD SAKS
Kevin	PATRICK MURRAY
Gary	STEPHEN PETCHER
Darryl	DANIEL WEBB

Directed by Antonia Bird
Designed by Roger Glossop
Costumes by Jane Harding
Lighting by Hugh Laver
Sound by Peter Deacon

CHARACTERS

COMMANDER DRISS, 48
RAINE, 26
ALICE, 21
BEVERLEY, 22
GARY, 19
KEVIN, 19
DARRYL, 23
FIRESTONE, 24
DOUG, 25

ACT ONE

The bus is a single decker. Bench seats up front. Emergency exit at the back is blocked up, with bars. Passenger/driver seat is placed in front of the main door exit which opens on to stage rear. The windows are whited out. There is a lavatory closet at the back facing the audience.

Lying on a bench seat is a khaki-sacked two/way talkie.

For non-naturalistic purposes it is to provide proper headroom. In the distance we can hear the carnival floats and bands and folk in large numbers.

We are placed below the Acklam Road bridge on Portobello Road. It is the second day, i.e. the main day of the carnival in Notting Hill Gate.

> [*The door opens from the outside. The illusion of a thin* CROWD *and shuffle of feet outside in the road.* COMMANDER DRISS'S VOICE *from where he stands outside the bus –*]

DRISS'S VOICE: . . . Let's 'ave yar! Morning girls! Upsie tupsie!

> [RAINE *climbs in with her case.* RAINE *wears WRAC (SGT) uniform.* ALICE *and* BEVERLEY *follow. They wear WPC uniforms. They carry their cases. The door is pulled shut from the outside. The air brake gives a hiss.*
> BEVERLEY *finds a wall thermometer, taps it.*]

BEV: Hot, init? . . . Eighty it says only eighty.

RAINE: We all talk in centigrade now. Corps Regulations.

BEV: Oh, yeh.

RAINE: Fahrenheit's been downgraded to non-usage.

BEV: Shame, init? . . . my brain still functions in fahrenheit.

RAINE: Keep up with the changes.

ALICE: I don't like changes much either.

BEV: But you know, Sarge, now that all me thinking is in fahrenheit like, I just can't seem to change it. I don't look up at the sky in the morning an' say, oh dear, it's down to six degrees. I say to meself, blimey, it's forty degrees and my bra's on the washing line frozen like a pair of rock cakes, Sarge.

ALICE: Me too, Sarge. I wouldn't put it like that.

RAINE: It's er – Alice and Beverley? Right.

BEV: WPC Beverley Watkin, Sarge.

ALICE: WPC Alice Heilbron, Sarge.

RAINE: Senior staff at the Norwich barracks call me Raine.

ALICE: Raine.

BEV: It's ... Bev, actually,

RAINE: All right, Bev. Now, you two have known each other before.

ALICE: Then I was moved to another station.

BEV: See, Sarge, Alice here always gets the soft jobs, because I'm big, they keep me for the rowdies like.

RAINE: You'd like the Women's Royal Army, Bev. Sounds like your ticket. None of this legging it round Piccadilly looking for pinpricks in teeny elbows. Or midnight panda rambles for car meter thieves. Anyway, we've got a job to do here, today. Job of joint operations. Right?

ALICE: Yes, Raine.

RAINE: Good girl.

BEV: Oh, Alice is a good girl. You know when I first met her she was doing football night volunteer duty. And she was so green she was still wearing suspenders under her uniform ...

ALICE: It was a nervous error, that was all.

BEV: Seriously, Sarge, there she was in a punch-up with two paddy tarts outside Euston station. And she lost her skirt.

ALICE: She's being very unfair.

BEV: And the football young shits from Scotland were pissing themselves something sodden. And there was Alice, mauve suspenders, lemony knickers, and stockings, trying to climb a ladder to get her skirt back. The rowdies had tossed her skirt on the diesel roof of the Midnight Glasgow Express.

ALICE: Truth to tell – it's my skin.

RAINE: Your skin?

BEV: Rule number one, women's police handbook, never

wear suspenders when on duty. They can be used against you in an aggressive manner.

ALICE: It's very sensitive.

BEV: And never ever put your knickers over your panty hose. Meaning – it is not easy to arrest an eight-foot-tall Aussie with twenty Foster pints down him on the Earls Court Road when your knickers have suddenly clanged to the floor.

ALICE: It is a strange fact even tight swimming costumes fetch me out in a rash. I think I'm allergic to interference with my body.

RAINE: That's all right, Alice.

BEV: When Alice goes out with a bloke she puts stickers on her skin where he can touch her and where he can't.

ALICE: Not true at all.

RAINE: What you ought to do, Alice, is to put talcum powder under things like bras.

ALICE: Oh I do. It doesn't help.

RAINE: Or go without bras at all.

ALICE: I couldn't do that.

BEV: Women's police handbook insists you wear a bra.

ALICE: Even if it didn't . . .

BEV: It's just Alice's nervous constitution.

ALICE: I don't really like to talk about it . . . you know if I do fancy a bloke . . . if I really do . . . a heat rash comes up all over my chest.

RAINE: We ought to start, girls. What have you got?

[*They place their individual cases and commence taking out garments.* RAINE *gives the lead. The two WPCs follow suit. They are methodical and specific.* ALICE *places herself discreetly so as not to be too much on display.*]

ALICE [*licking pencil too*]: Blouse from the War-on-Want shop, very cheap, bit tight, a pound. Skirt from the *Release Chilean Prisoners* old clothes raffle corner of Marble Arch last Sunday. Pound fifty. And daft cloggies from a pile of leftovers we picked up after the Anti-Nazi League Rally. Awful lot of *them* must have gone home without shoes. It is how they're brought up, they bring *them* up like that and that's what turns *them* into *them*. Total – two pound fifty.

RAINE: Your handbag?

[ALICE *snaps her fingers as if to remind herself. She pulls out her bag from the case. It is capacious and possesses a ritzy patina.*]

BEV: Anything in it?

ALICE: One regulation whistle and a pair of handcuffs.

RAINE: Alice, you'll need some cash in it otherwise what have you got *him* for? A tenpenny whistle and a pair of discarded knick-knacks?

ALICE: I could put my own purse in it, couldn't I?

BEV: Very good, Alice.

RAINE: How are you going to wave that bag around?

ALICE [*swings it*]: Loosen the clasp here . . . let it seem half-way open . . .

BEV: And swing it hard. All about.

RAINE: Bev?

BEV: Half a dozen safety pins. Forget that. Day glow satin top done with shock sequins. Nine quid eighty. Fantastic studded belt with amazing Nazi effect. Four quid nineteen. Insane tight deep split Rita Hayworth skirt with monster badges. Skirt seven. Inhuman dazzle colour tights three somfin. Captain Speed rollers did a borrer I did from me kid brother.

ALICE: How can you possibly get around in a mob of *them* on rollers?

BEV: I keep on the fringe. Soon as I see *them* at it I'm faster on me rollers than hoofing it, aren't I? I can provide quick alert in no time. Plus mind you plus a pair of Nazi SS daggers do a dangle from me belt. How much you think them cost?

ALICE: Cost a fortune!

BEV: Staff sergeant lent me it all. He'd got a personal collection in his front-room glass cabinet. I've seen it all.

ALICE: He's got three kids and a wife you know . . .

BEV: He and me did a Come Dancing duo in the Federation Ball, last year. He's got a very nifty foxtrot when his regulation patent leathers don't warble. And as for his Mexican Tango – I've never bent over backwards so far for any man in my life –

ALICE: – Painful, is it? –

BEV: – And that's why – you taking a rise out of me, Alice, are you?

RAINE: How much, Bev?

BEV: Ah ... er ... £32.99p.

ALICE: Beverley Watkin!

BEV: Something wrong, Alice Heilbron?

ALICE: I spent less than a fiver! You can't knock up a fortune just because you done two how's your father tangos with the staff sergeant and you've heard his patent leather pumps warble!

BEV: I'm worth £32.99p to me I am. That is for sure.

[*Pause.*

THE THREE GIRLS *lounge on the bunk seat.* RAINE *puts away the sachet. The outside door swings open. We hear* DRISS'S VOICE. *Three very youthful-looking* SQUADDIES *bundle in. Each carries a haversack loaded, and each sack contains a curved shield-like object. And a broad stick.*
Street noises.

GARY *and* KEVIN *and* DARRYL. DARRYL *is the eldest by a few years. Has a CPL stripe.* KEVIN *seems too young. Taut and naïve. It is* GARY *who fancies anything that moves. It is* DARRYL *who has had the genuine experience in Belfast.*

They park themselves. The GIRLS *move away. The state of the* GIRLS' *undress makes them gawp.*

The GIRLS *ignore them and finish their ready-reckoning.*]

BEV: Time and a half is all we get on both days you know. Bloody union Trot gets twice and a half and a big kiss just for signing on in any normal job. I think even the Khaki gets more'n we do, Alice. I'm the new poor I am.

RAINE: You girls get London Living Allowance Rating. I don't.

BEV: But you get fully paid up bread an' board for coming down from Norwich, Raine? An' three meals, an' travel, an' incidentals.

RAINE: Don't argue with me, Bev. I'm adding up your whack. Thirty-two knicker in your hand. Thirteen knicker day allowance. Plus time and a half knicker. You've got forty-five knickers and I can't see sunshine through thirty knickers.

GARY/DARRYL: Excuse me!

GARY: Funny thing – I can't see more'n three knickers from here. Excuse me!

DARRYL: Excuse him!

GARY: What do you say, Kevin?

KEVIN: Eh?...

GARY: Never mind the sunshine!

KEVIN: What?...

BEV [to RAINE]: Everybody in the army gets top rate City Waiting Allowance.

RAINE: Every year, the Review Board pipes up – can we have a little bit more please? We can't even apply to Equal Opportunities for help. No one speaks for us, Beverley. All that notion you've got is a lot of old cock.

DARRYL: Oi! Excuse us, won't you!

GARY: I don't want to put a damper on it like. But you've embarrassed my pal here with all this knickers and old cock bit.

RAINE [noticing him at last]: What?

GARY: Er, knickers and old cocks and that –

RAINE: Go on, lad, put your Y-fronts back in your mouth will you.

GARY [to DARRYL]: I like it!

DARRYL: Definitely!

GARY: Kev?

KEVIN: Oh no...

GARY [to RAINE]: Look, love ... I don't know what you're doing in here, but this is a Special Services bus. Detailed for Special Services Observation and Enforcement Procedures. It isn't the boating lido on the Serpentine, you know.

RAINE: I think he's trying to say something to us.

GARY: You all been picked up by Old Bill? That it? What you been doin' – bit of trade for the tourists, was it?

DARRYL: Naughty girls, you.

GARY: And the Law come up in a panda and called you in? Oh you bad girls, you. You don't want to be left alone in a bus with a bunch of khaki like us. You know what they say about us lot in our camp – it ain' 'all out' like unions, it's 'all off', that's what we say, 'all off', Darryl, init?

DARRYL: Take 'em all off.

RAINE [to BEV]: Do you think he's finished?

BEV: I don't know. He's got quite a big mouth, there might be some more to come out.

GARY: Wake up, Kev, then!

KEVIN: ... Yes!

GARY: Here, Kev, I fancy mine, but I don't fancy yours! Do you fancy yours, Darryl?

DARRYL: I'm still choosing.

GARY [to RAINE]: It's Darryl you see – he's slow and very polite. It's pools, init? It's three Draws, Darryl, init? Three Draws.

ALICE [to GIRLS]: It's interesting when they think they're funny.

GARY: S'all right, Kev, I'll explain it next week!

KEVIN: Oh ta ...

RAINE [to KEVIN]: He means it's like choosing the Three Draws Football Coupon. Geddit?

KEVIN: I ... don't need you to tell me, thank you.

GARY: Go on in there, Kev! That's it! All off! Right?

RAINE [to the GIRLS]: If Alice would take one end of this blanket, and Bev this end. I think we'll make a bit of privacy. Don't you?

[RAINE *takes a large rolled blanket and the girls pin it across the back third portion of the bus.*

KEVIN *starts to take off his boots and his jacket.*]

RAINE: Help put a pin here ... right ...

[*And* GARY *goes up close to the blanket. The girls on the other side.*]

GARY: Look out, girls ... old Kevin's taking his clothes off ...

DARRYL: Feeling the heat now ... Kevin's got his shirt off ... his pants have gone ...

GARY: You can see the funny colour the whites of his eyes have gone. There's that manic nuttynut-nut look on his mouth. His jaw is setting tight. And he's grinding his teeth. Wooorr, Kev . . . I can't hold him back. He's bulging all over the place in funny places. Look out! He's coming!

[GARY *has taken a running header through the curtain with a suitable cry. The girls have finished fixing the blanket. They watch with disinterested fascination as* GARY *charges to the end of their side of the bus. Bangs himself on the back wall. Reaches for the closet door and hurls himself inside. And commences a noisy wanking banging send-up. Knees and elbows hammering until the bus seems to shake.* GARY *adds a few grunts and gasps. The girls stare nonplussed. Very still.*

DARRYL *lies on his back and kicks his legs in the air.*

KEVIN *stares dourly at* DARRYL. DARRYL *is cycling his legs in the air.*]

DARRYL: . . . Come on, Kev!

KEVIN: Is Gary all right?

DARRYL: Get down here and wave your legs in the air, you idiot, like me!

KEVIN: What is Gary doing?

DARRYL: He's in the bog doing a big wank, what do you think he's doing, Christ! Come on!

[KEVIN *won't.*]

KEVIN: You see . . . Darryl . . . I don't really think it's funny at all, I'm sorry, Darryl.

[DARRYL *stops.* GARY *stops.* GARY *emerges from the closet.* KEVIN *stands up. As* GARY *walks back through the curtain.*]

. . . Sorry, Gary.

[GARY *and* DARRYL *and* KEVIN *sit on the bench.* GARY *and* DARRYL *take off their tunics and loosen the shirts beneath.* KEVIN *is suddenly quiet beside them.*

BEV *and* ALICE *have slipped on shirts/blouses. They step through the curtain. They watch the silent boys.*

RAINE *steps from behind the blanket wearing her uniform jacket. The Sgt. stripes are visible. It is loosely buttoned.*

She stands there. DARRYL *looks up. He nudges* GARY. *Who eventually looks up.*]

RAINE [*not unpleasant*]: Stand up, boys.

[GARY *looks closer with amazement. He and* KEVIN *and* DARRYL *do as they're told. Unfortunately* DARRYL'*s trousers have been loosened with his belt undone and the pants slip.* DARRYL *is about to hitch them up.*]

Stand straight . . .

[DARRYL'*s pants do fall down.*]

Name and rank and station?

GARY [*big breath*]: Simpkin. Gary. Private. Royal Fusiliers, Worcester Barracks, Special Detail.

DARRYL: Henshall. Darryl. Lance Corporal, 17th Field Infantry, Leeds Lineham Camp, Special Detail.

KEVIN: Reynolds. Kevin Arnold. Private. Royal Fusiliers, Worcester Training Barracks, Worcester Shrub Hill, Special Detail.

RAINE: Is there . . . something wrong with your trousers, Henshall?

DARRYL [*hitching up*]: No. Nothing wrong at all.

RAINE: Stand easy . . . now shall we straighten ourselves out. This is WPC Beverley Watkin. This is WPC Alice Heilbron. Both attached to the London Metropolitan Police. Paddington and Maida Vale districts. I am Sergeant Lorraine Hollinsloe. Women's Royal Army Corps. Ordinance Group designated C for Charlie S for sugar and U for umpire, Counter Surveillance Unit, Tinbar Dale Women's Camp, Norwich. And none of us is being held in this vehicle for any activities connected with looking for trade amongst tourists.

GARY: Permission to speak?

RAINE: Of course.

GARY: Permission to apologize?

RAINE: No call for that.

GARY: With all due respect – I wasn't expecting to find the sergeant inside the bus on duty standing in her knickers and brassière in pursuance of partaking of a conversation with her fellow officers about old cocks and Y-fronts.

RAINE: We were changing our clothes.

GARY: Furthermore, I was led to be understood that while whereas we were placed under the requirements of Special Duty orders, and were required to foregather at 14.00 hours at the juncture of Acklam Road and Portobello Road, London, Notting Hill Gate, in this military bus, we were not led to be told that as it was joint security effort nobody would pull rank on anybody else, Sergeant.

RAINE: Thank you, Gary, for that speech. I quite agree. We are here, like you, to take orders from the Commander when he appears. I won't pull rank. I'll pull sex. Perhaps you haven't noticed it – but we are three women. OK? Shake?

[*She shakes his hand.* BEV *shakes* DARRYL's *hand.* ALICE *is hesitant. But shakes* KEVIN's *hand. He keeps his eyes low.*]

RAINE [*to* GARY]: No hard feelings then?

GARY: I wouldn't say that. Would you, Darryl?

DARRYL: *Hard* feelings? You got your *hard* feelings ain't yer, Kev? Kev's got his still! It's the heat!

KEVIN [*to* ALICE]: I'm not like these two. I've got soft feelings as well.

ALICE: I'm Alice.

KEVIN: Kev.

ALICE: Hallo, Kev.

BEV: Duty first, Alice!

[*The door opens again. More music. The sense of light and heat outside and fresh air and movement outside.*

ALICE *and* KEVIN *study each other. But* BEV *pulls* ALICE *back behind the curtain with* RAINE *as another figure climbs in. He is black and young and in informal gear. He carries a plastic suit zipper with the pressed suit inside it and a small valise/soft bag. The girls have gone behind the curtain. They pin a second rug across a back seat and we see less of them.*

GARY *and* DARRYL *and* KEVIN *stare at the arrival. The door shuts on them. Street sounds recede. The music is still there in our ears. And closer.*

The new arrival is FIRESTONE BONNELLA. *If possible he*

should be taller than the lads. And a little older. He wears a
regulation blue shirt under his jacket.

FIRESTONE *sets about changing his clothes. He kicks off*
his things and lays out the police uniform which is inside the
plastic zipper. He fetches a helmet out of his soft bag. The
lads begin to gawp.]

FIRESTONE: Afternoon, lads . . . [*Silence.*] Hot enough for
you ? . . . [*Silence.*] Big day today, right ? . . . [*Silence.*]

DARRYL: Coventry home to Liverpool, Gary ?

GARY: 2–4, Liverpool. Any day. Norwich home to Chelsea ?

DARRYL: Draw ?

GARY: O K. Draw.

FIRESTONE [*changing*]: You like football ? What do you think
of West Brom ?

DARRYL [*to* GARY]: England–New Zealand, Gary ?

GARY: Rests mainly whether Boycott can repeat those cen-
turies he did earlier in the year, don't it . . . too easy knock-
ing birds out the trees in Pakistan . . . it's different here.

DARRYL: What's missing in the English team is a sense of –

FIRESTONE: I like cricket. I watch it. You play it ? . . .

GARY: Do you know anything about greyhound racing,
Darryl ?

FIRESTONE: Name's Firestone. Firestone Bonnella. I'm
from Dalston. Murder to get here today. Top train from
the Junction to Liverpool Street. Take the Circle because
they closed the Central Line because of the crowds.
Taking the Circle takes twice as long. And I should have
checked in half an hour ago. Checked in here, like. Name's
Firestone . . . ?

KEVIN [*silence, then*]: . . . Kevin.

FIRESTONE: How are you, Kevin ?

KEVIN: Not so bad.

GARY [*to* KEVIN]: Oh no, you're not. You've begun to get
moony since you got here. You was all right when we met
up at the station. All right until you come in here. All of a
sudden – you've turned against your only friend Gary.
Gary who's been your companion through thick and thin
on the journey down from Worcester, Gary who rescued

23

you half-sick with Newcastle Brown Ale and about to fall down the British Rail lav pan so I heard.

KEVIN: What have I done wrong?

DARRYL: I know it's difficult for you to understand, Kev, but in the army first rule is don't open up your trap to anyone until you know they is trustworthy and reliable, secret of camp communication is never give a stranger an even break until –

FIRESTONE: Until you find out first he's not going to kick your balls off whilst you ain' looking.

GARY: Did I hear someone?

FIRESTONE: Just what we learn in the Police Federation Academy at Watling. Firestone's the name.

GARY: Excuse me and I don't think that we've ever been introduced, excuse me –

FIRESTONE: You're Gary, are you? You're Darryl? Me – Firestone!

GARY: Frankly, it is not much skin off my nose whether your name is Firestone or Dunlop. Do you mind?

[FIRESTONE *slips into blue regular trousers and reaches for the police jacket.*]

FIRESTONE: You doing Special Duties? Me, too, man.

GARY: Oh, yes? Special Duty Tree Branch surveillance, is it?

FIRESTONE: That's right. My job is to hang in the trees and do a Tarzan job from one end of Ladbroke Grove to the top of Notting Hill, scratching my armpits you know and cracking hazelnuts. You got the idea.

DARRYL: What Special Duty then?

[FIRESTONE *holds up his jacket.*]

FIRESTONE: Ordinary copper's duty.

GARY: Who you kidding? Today? Out there?

FIRESTONE: I was deputed here by Publicity and Information 'P' Department, with the agreement of my station Detective Inspector. My brief is to walk around smiling at as many people I can and to keep as close as possible to press photographers and TV news cameras, to ensure maximum coverage. Did you never see me in those Anti-Nazi League Rallies? I was upfront helping a pregnant girl hold up her banner, she was almost fainting – it said 'END FASCIST PIG CORRUPTION'. For the past two years, I always get sent up to the Labour Party Conference at Blackpool. I get ten days' leave with holiday pay and a hotel bedroom on the front. All I have to do is open Mr Merlyn Rees's Rover car door each time he arrives outside a building for a speech you know. And he gets out of the car, gives me a cheery wave, and runs in through the crowd.

GARY: Excuse me, I am impressed, I am!

FIRESTONE: That got me the front page spread on the Labour Party Law and Immigration manifesto last Christmas. Me and Merlyn that was. Us together. And I been with the Queen too.

GARY: A goer, is she? It's a wonder you ain' on the front cover of *Woman's Own* every week.

FIRESTONE: If you watch the box carefully – every time the royal coach drives into the yard of Parliament Buildings, the day she's doing her Queen's speech bit, and she's waving out of the coach to the idiots – we always call those foreigners the idiots – they'd trample each other to death if it wasn't for us – just as she reaches the gate to the yard, there I am. Right in front of the BBC TV news camera team. Sometimes the cameraman asks me to put a bit of colour into the scene for him, before she comes, so I stamp about a bit on the idiots' feet I'm holding back behind me. That makes them fall over and hang on to my legs. Gets quite good then. I've been twice in the *Illustrated London News*. Last carnival, I got into the *Daily Mail* centre page pic doing a dance with one of the West Indian beauty queens on them floats.

DARRYL: Costs a fortune all this make up, don't it?

FIRESTONE: I'm black, mate, I am.

GARY: Wonder you find time – half-inching your way up and down in the countryside in the company of ministers and royals day and night – wonder it is you can find your way back to Dalston for an honest day's work.

KEVIN [*to* FIRESTONE]: Firestone what?

FIRESTONE: Bonnella.

KEVIN: Firestone Bonnella?

FIRESTONE: My dad is Italian. He come from the south and was done by the British army – the whole column surrendered. There were no facilities for a POW camp and they shipped him to England. My mother come later. After the war was over. He had a British work permit by then.

KEVIN: Italian? Both of them?

FIRESTONE: They were Abyssinians really. But they came to Italy from North Africa to fulfil this demand for cheap labour. In them days Mussolini thought he owned Abyssinia. So he declared war against it, and somehow sort of lost the war. And it became Ethiopia. Then he joined up with the Nazis, and he lost that war too. So after it was all over, the whole Brindisi coastline was full of Black Italian Ethiopians with nowhere to go and nothing to do. That was me Mum and Dad.

GARY: It just strikes me – what was the point in getting inside without your uniform on just now then, excuse me – ?

FIRESTONE: Did you think I could get from central London to Notting Hill Gate in one piece in a copper's twinset on a day like this?

DARRYL: What's the difference now? You ain' going to sit in here blacking up your boots, are you?

FIRESTONE: No. I'm relying on you. You're the army, ain't you? Well then . . .

GARY: You mean you're going to step out there when the time comes and stay with the other police?

FIRESTONE: Give and take.

GARY: Well why don't you bloody start at the Ladbroke Grove Police Station with the rest of them then?

FIRESTONE: I . . . got my reasons.

GARY: You have?

FIRESTONE: I like it here. I . . . like the action.

GARY: In a Police Personnel Carrier like this?

FIRESTONE: That's . . . right.

GARY: Wiv us? Who are you pullin' the leg of!

FIRESTONE: I . . . have my reasons.

GARY: Who am pullin' the leg, like!

FIRESTONE: Don't lip me, lad. If I say I do I do. This was the Personnel Carrier I chose. An' this was the agreement with my Station Officer. An' so don't lip me, see . . . it is only a job, right? Doin' me duty, right?

GARY: I do not believe you.

FIRESTONE: I am happy doing my work.

KEVIN: No, you ain'.

FIRESTONE [*sudden*]: What do you know, pin-head?

GARY: Hallo. Something Kev said got under the belt there.

KEVIN: I was only saying I didn't think –

FIRESTONE: Don't! OK?

> [BEV *comes out from behind the extra side-on rug/curtain. She is wearing her lurid punk outfit. Very odd decorations on her face and arms. Nazi badges and totem items. She has a handful of safety pins. She comes through the dividing curtain into the bench area where the boys are with* FIRESTONE. *They sit there in glum silence. Taking no attention of her. Icy atmosphere.*]

BEV: What's the matter? Cheer up, fellas, this is meant to be Carnival Day, not World War Three. Tea without milk? Tea without sugar? No? . . . that's a relief 'cos there's only tea with! Didn't your family pack you a sandwich box, then?

FIRESTONE: I don't have a family. And I don't eat sandwiches.

BEV: Darryl, d'you want to help me pin on me safety pins?

DARRYL: On where?

BEV: Anywhere I can't reach myself.

GARY: And there's plenty of that, darling!

BEV: You watch it! Pin it, I said.

DARRYL: You never asked if I was married, Bev.

BEV: I know you're not married.

> [*The door opens and the street sounds are loud here.* DRISS's *voice is outside. And the messiest-looking lank hippy trogs up the steps of the bus. Long and dishevelled hair. Extravagant Vietnam war-being out of sync with the day. Shambling container of nouveau nostalgic semiotics. He is* DOUG. *Older than the lads.*]

27

DRISS'S VOICE: You been in the river all night? Fumigate fumigate! Get on!

[*The door closes on them. The street music is near but far. On the horizon of the ears. Not an echo any longer.*

The lads do a bit of sniffing as DOUG *enters. He sits opposite* GARY. *Sniff sniff sound.*]

GARY: Hallo, it must be something in the breeze? What do you say, Kev?

KEVIN: I've always had blocked sinuses speaking for myself.

DARRYL: Kev's lucky. It's like London drains done a tidal down Portobello Market.

BEV [*leaving with a smile and a wriggle*]: Excuse me. I'll safety pin the rest of meself up now.

DARRYL [*touching his nose, nod and wink toward* DOUG]: Sniff sniff . . . don't yer wan' a pin through yer nose keep the drarft aht?

[DOUG *leans back and searches in his pockets. He seems at a loss to find anything.*]

DOUG: Got some skins on you?

GARY: Skins?

DOUG: Yearh, skins –

GARY: Only skin I got, chummy, I'm wearing.

DOUG: Don't give me a hard time. I was goin' to light up. We've got a few minutes.

GARY: I've got no intention of giving you a 'hard time', friend. Excuse me.

[DOUG *eventually finds a packet of cigarette papers. Now he is looking for something else. And what is more he cannot seem to find it.*]

DOUG: As a matter of fact you could do yourself a favour if you threw me a handful of weed, man. Weed, man, you know like – Old Walter Raleigh used to call tobacco.

GARY: Excuse me, I still do call it tobacco, excuse me.

[DOUG *has lost something else.* DARRYL *and* GARY *and* FIRESTONE *are riveted to the search amongst* DOUG's *grisly pockets.* DOUG *searches and searches.*

But DOUG *fetches out a silver wrapped wad of tobacco and breathes a sigh of relief. Now he's back inside his pockets searching again.*]

DOUG: Jeezus . . . I think I've lost my shit, oh bad scene, man. How could I be so dumb?

GARY [*looking along the floor*]: So long as you haven't lost it on the floor when you come in sniff sniff sniff I don't give a piss in the ocean.

DOUG [*locates a brown nugget*]: It's all right . . . no sweat, man . . . everything's holy, man . . .

> [DOUG *takes out a pocket knife and asks* FIRESTONE *to hold it.* DOUG *fetches out a lighter and heats the knife. He gently takes the knife and slices and scrapes the brown nugget. He balances papers and tobacco and shit on his knees. Very wobbly.*]

. . . Thank you, man. Thank you, man, right on, man.

> [FIRESTONE *stares dully.*]

DOUG [*rolls the worst-looking joint anyone has ever seen. He takes his time about it*]: . . . Bad scene all the way here, you know . . . like nothing but hundreds and hundreds of blue helmet honks and pigs . . . sussing you out. . . . tossing the Sus Laws at anyone and everyone, you know . . . like they bloody owned the streets, you know . . . always a strip off for the chicks, too, man. Coming on heavy like 'We have reason to believe you got ten ounces of shit placed inside your knickers, darlin'.' Bloody aggro spreadin' it like butter gone suddenly out of fashion. Fuck 'em, you know, give me William Blake deep throat love an' peace, man. William Blake said all humanity is to be taken with a pinch of salt (or something he said or something) . . . id and ying come together . . . I was in a *real* pub the other day with straights, you know, had to force myself to drink a half pint of brown ale (alcohol puts back the stress in your body your organic meditation has taken out, you know) and I was watching them play darts on the wall. I went up to this Irish brother playing. I told him, man, if he blindfolded himself and did a deep karma therapy and placed the mystic dart-board in the centre of his all-seeing zen eye deep inside his head he'd hit the treble twenties so often, you know, the fucking darts would grow karma angel zen maintenance spirit wings. But he was just programmed into alcoholized brown water, you know, and then he poured a whole pint of it over my head.

[DOUG *has completed this joint in between his fingers. It flops loosely all over the place. Bits either end. And rightly it does look like –*]

GARY [*pause*]: . . . . That . . . without doubt is the worst most cock and bull roll-up. Excuse me.

DOUG: Don't put me down, man –

DARRYL: Put you down, yer long-haired dose of undiluted mystical hippy moo talk, put you where?!

DOUG [*standing and yelling*]: Don't lay your bad vibrations on my karma Blake peace scene, man!

GARY: Pathetic. You couldn't roll a greased ball-bearing down a one-in-two slope, mate!

DOUG [*slight change in his voice, the slangy quality goes*]: I was only kidding, soldier.

GARY: What am I, an idiot?

FIRESTONE: It's all right – he was just taking you for a bit of a ride. He's a member of –

GARY: You keep out of this. We don't want no condescending black lip from your lip, excuse me!

FIRESTONE [*to* GARY]: It's all right, stoopid. He's only tryin' you on. He's only givin' you a bit of a piss up, you can take piss up, can't yer? He's pointin' out the fact you are just a silly little bit of khaki noggins, an' he's takin' the rise. OK?

GARY: All of a sudden you've become the know-all. I know a little know-all guess-all about you I do. Don't try to pretend you've got something over us because we're just khaki. I've a bit of know-all about you, too. There's a bloody good reason why you told Bev there you ain' got no family. Shall we say you ain' got no family at all to live with because your family took one look at the sort of blue uniform you've got yourself grassed up into and suddenly they didn't want to know, did they? Who was it down the local street turn round and say piss off now, Firestone boy, you're a turn-coat you are. And then who was it perhaps somewhere else – auntie or uncle or was it a girl you kind of liked? Good-bye, Firestone, you've changed football team, have you, so cheery-bye. And then what else we got?

FIRESTONE: You're going too far –

GARY: There was that little sir echo about the other police in Paddington Central or Ladbroke Grove was it? Funny you never bothered your hide to check in there with them before you come to us in this bus. Why was that?

FIRESTONE: I'll break you, boy . . . !

GARY: Something something er to do with on account nobody down there in those police stations wants to see you walk in their door. Nobody wants the pleasure of seeing you walk around in one of their uniforms. Suddenly it looks to them like one of *them* outside *them* taking the mickeytake. Isn't that the truth? Police don't want one of *them* outside *them* dressed up in a blue uniform. What's in it for them? Nothing at all. Can they crack their woggy and their yiddy jokes in the changing room whilst you're putting Kiwi boot polish on? Course they can't. And what are they supposed to do when you go out in a file with them? Are they supposed to act mother and father to you when brother comes up? Funny acting mother and father to likes of you when your own kith bloody disowned you and threw you out of the house funny, excuse me!

DOUG [*to* FIRESTONE]: What do you think?

FIRESTONE: Why not.

[DOUG *and* FIRESTONE *with very deft and professional moves lay both* DARRYL *and* GARY *out on the floor of the bus.* KEVIN *makes a sort of daft move towards them and* FIRESTONE *almost lifts* KEVIN *into the air.* KEVIN *crouches in a heap at the bottom of the bus. Does his best to wriggle out of trouble by hiding beneath* DARRYL *and* GARY. DARRYL *and* GARY *are howling now. As the boots go in. And there is nothing they can do. They are stuck in the bottom like three sardines. Tightly packed. All* THREE GIRLS *come out of the back curtain and help the boys on the floor. They show an unexpected warmth and concern.* DOUG *and* FIRESTONE *stand off.* DARRYL *and* GARY *slowly pull themselves to their feet and dust their bruises.* KEVIN *is still lying on the ground moaning but nobody seems to have touched him particularly.*]

KEVIN: . . . Oh don't . . . don't . . . !

[ALICE *kneels there and strokes his head. What looks a trifle funny in* KEVIN *clearly now is not. There is a painful and vulnerable quality about him.*

BEV *and* RAINE *help* DARRYL *and* GARY. *They keep themselves noticeably in between the other two –* FIRESTONE *and* DOUG. BEV *and* RAINE *act as shields just in case the fight starts up again. As it almost does –*]

GARY [*to* DOUG *and* FIRESTONE]: You're not supposed to hit Kevin. He's got a sensitive constitution.

FIRESTONE: You're lucky I'm leaving you alive!

DARRYL [*certain bravura in front of* BEV *and* DOUG]: If you hadn't have taken us like that by surprise, I would have done for you, so help me.

DOUG [*cold and clinical*]: With a thumb . . . that . . . I could break your eardrum like a peapod.

[*The* GIRLS *are not yet fully dressed. They have towels around their waists and shirts loosely flapping with the exception of* BEV *whose hair is now a very bright colour indeed.*

RAINE *is helpful to* GARY *and brushes his hair back for him.* BEV *does the same for* DARRYL.

ALICE *sits beside* KEVIN *on the floor.*]

ALICE [*whispers*]: . . . I'm glad you're sensitive, Kev.

KEVIN: If my nerves get jangled it says it says on the report sheet in my billet – I can positively lose control.

[BEV *and* DARRYL. DARRYL *smiles and nods.*]

BEV: Come on, Darryl, finish off me safety pins?

[DOUG *and* FIRESTONE. FIRESTONE *grins as* DOUG *puts his arms round him in Come Dancing fashion.*]

DOUG [*girlish*]: There you go – yer big beefy number you – what's it to be, foxtrot or quickstep?

[*The door opens. The outside penetrates. Noise from the street. The floats and the singing and the drums and the shuffle of feet somewhere close by. That little bit closer. Louder on the ears.*

COMMANDER DRISS *steps up and closes the door carefully behind him. Unusual man perhaps in his late forties. Dressed in a suitable Cirencester market-day farming outfit,*

*leather patches on elbows and discreet NFU-type lapel
badge and a club tie.*

All BUS INMATES *stiffen up no end as* DRISS *enters.*]

DRISS: V glad to see you all lads and lassies coming along
chummy. Stiffen up a bit now. The Scots shit-house
governor is among you and wants your attention. Driss is
the name, D for Driss. No time for first names. Commander,
former Argyll and Sutherland Highlanders Security and
Communication Grouping. Drafted out of the Argylls and
placed under M.I.6. Queen Street civvy land with C for
Commander status, and further drafted on to the Special
Air Service Regiment, Bradbury Lines, Hereford, where
I am a first year instructor in counter operations. Settle
down now, I'm going to give you a little talk. Now, what
are we all doing here in these Special Duty rendezvous, and
what are we all doing mixing oil and water and wine with
different Her Majesty departments? We are all doing this
in accordance with an over-riding Ministry of Defence
White Paper, which, last year, made the recommendation
that all forces of Law and Order, L for Law, O for Order,
should from time to time foregather in harmonic displays
of combined ops. Now, whether or not the purists among
us agree with this decision, it is something little monkeys
like all of our serving ilk must follow to the letter, nevertheless. Now ...

[DRISS *studies* DOUG, *curiously.*]

DOUG [*stiffly*]: Detective Sergeant Hailwood, sir. Tulse Hill
Police Station, Thurlestone Road, London S.E.27. Newly
attached to the Special Patrol Group (SPG, sir), with specific instructions in pursuance of the 1824 Vagrancy Act, to
enforce new Metropolitan guidelines as regards the Act, sir.

[GARY's *eyes wide on* DOUG.]

DRISS: The operative words are Counter Surveillance. You
all have been seconded here under Ministry of Defence
Special Duties Combined Operations. This is a new scheme
to put into motion all departments of Law and Order when
the situation should arise. And in terms of legality, it is an
experiment in combined ops to unite officers who would

normally not be working side by side. As far as the Min. of
D for Defence is concerned, it is a useful function of
modern warfare to see how events relating to the Civil
Disobedience Acts, the suppression of Terrorism Acts, and
the Vagrancy Acts can be tackled by means of a cross-
pollenization of forces. Each Ministry of Defence bus has
to work as a cell alone. Each bus is strategically placed along
the route of the carnival march today. Each bus has these
whited-out windows for a medical effect. Each bus, as you
will have noticed, bears the sign 'Royal Borough of Kensington and Chelsea Child Immunization Mobile Dis-
pensary'. And certain buses are placed at junctions of high
density egress, should the bands and floats and accompany-
ing types break out of a controlled route and run mad dog
on us. The high density junctions for sudden and wilful
egress are in themselves closely sealed with police barriers,
dogs, and cycle police. Naturally, those assorted types who
take part in the march are obliged to demonstrate their
carnival spirit within this pre-arranged route. Any devia-
tion of the spirit of carnival is strictly circumscribed. You
may take heart that we possess, on our side, a ten-year-old
horse, trained to a red-brick university standard, which can
lie down and pretend to be wounded by hordes of bovver
boy lefties.

[*He switches the two/way receiver.*]

[*Static chatter.*]

[*Switching out* CRACKLE VOICE.] This is Charley Tango
Bravo . . . this is Charley Tango Bravo . . . Partic Thistle,
please? Open line Partic Thistle?

[*He switches* CRACKLE VOICE *back.*]

[*Static chatter.*]

[*Switching out* CRACKLE VOICE.]: This is Charley Tango
Bravo . . . Hallo Partic Thistle?

[*Static chatter.*]

[DRISS *switches the two/way off, and places it back on a
seat.*]

Of course . . . in normal circumstances these gadgets work a
treat. It must be the sun outside affecting the wavelengths.

34

Or, more likely too many buggers have switched on their tellies to watch the carnival and the interference is dishing our batteries. That's the trouble with spectacles, it attracts too many itinerants, and there's not enough room left for the professionals. Where was I?

FIRESTONE: Tactics of high density egress control, sir.

DRISS: I want you to know what we are up against. There are over half a million of *them* outside. They have come from God knows what hole in the wall, and they are in full strength. There are additional tourists and curiosity flotsam. There are numerous radio and TV media link-ups out there. And the number of vehicles which converge on this area amount to an estimated eighty thousand cars parked in order to aggravate local police trafficking. On our side, we have four thousand police and policewomen from the Metropolitan and South East Areas. Also, we have a rough calculation of five hundred personnel, army and police and allied groups, who will monitor the march from beginning to end in normal plainclothes. In the main they will act as observers and in certain cases as counter-surveillance intelligence gatherers. The Ministry of Defence has I believe invited a few representatives of Law Enforcement from Munich, from Tokyo, and from Belfast and from Paris. But there is an interesting approach to the problem of mob control that the Ministry is at pains to demonstrate to these foreign types. That is that – although we are out-numbered one hundred to one by *them*, the climate we live in precludes the philosophy of over-kill. These foreign-type observers will not see hundreds of baton-wielding French froggy Algerian police laying into students and cracking skulls. They will see mob police control effectively containing the entire half million nosy parkers in one tightly packed route with no divergencies whatsoever. They will see small pockets of militarily armoured men take up positions of strength, but there will be no CS gas canister lobbing. The police have time and again begged the Ministry not to wave around CS gas, because this will only encourage the crowd to break and run. Exactly what is not

35

on the police menu today. CS canisters have to be worn.
They have to be seen to be worn. But their use is strictly
forbidden under an agreement between Ministry and Com-
missioner of Police. The operative words are – curtailment,
confinement, and restraint within boundaries, in order that
the rest of the decent population can proceed about their
ordinary business with the least possible interference from
the carnival instigators and their fellow travellers. Where
was I?

DOUG: Aspects of operative control, sir.

DRISS: Followed on by procedural control. How you will
proceed with your duties under the abnormal stress of half
a million of them as against five thousand of us. Consump-
tion of alcoholic beverages. All public houses have been
advised to close throughout the carnival two days. All off-
licences have been boarded up. The Council has agreed
with the Shopkeepers' Association to meet the bill for this.
All hotels and restaurants and clubs in the vicinity, up to but
not including the foreign street of Queensway, have been
advised about dispensing alcoholic beverages to anybody
who comes off the street for purchase of same. The advice
has come in the form of a Police letter reminding such
licensees of their opportunities in the future of renewing
drink licences. If we find any individual hawking illegal
alcohol in the disguise of Mister Softee ice cream carts, it is
our duty to apprehend on the spot.

BEV: Sir, if the suspect evades apprehension, what do we do?

DOUG: What I normally do is: advise him of his rights of
silence and due process, thereupon I kick his balls off and
stand on his head until I can attract the attention of a passing Panda.

DRISS: All local chemists and those chemist shops on a weekend rota have been advised to close. All garages have taken
the advice to empty forecourts of vehicles. All public
lavatories are closed under Council co-operation. Therefore any urinating in public places or private back gardens,
any defecating against walls, and any overt sexual acts
deemed to be –

36

DOUG: Public Order Act 1936, sir. Has 'em got by their short an' curlies, sir.

DRISS: Interesting act brought into effect to curtail Mosley Marchers. Now, all knives, wooden sticks, bricks and umbrellas come under the Offensive Weapons Act '74. All fighting that starts up between *themselves* comes under Affray and Intent to Cause Harm. All pickpocketing comes under Robbery with Violence. All snatched handbags come under same. Yes, Mr Hailwood?

DOUG [*motioning*]: It has been established in recent years that the Courts, the Magistrates' Courts that is, are prepared to buy offences caused by congregating in numbers thereby infringing the Vagrancy Law 1824, section two.

DRISS: How numerous must they be?

DOUG: Three or more, sir. Three or more come under Loitering with Intent under the Vagrancy one. It's a corker. Lewisham and Lambeth have been leading the way there no end, sir.

DRISS: Well done, Lambeth. Don't approach the carnival stewards or so-called marshals with armbands. The day will eventually deteriorate until they can control nothing and nobody. In that eventuality, one normally discovers that *them themselves* have had so many internal quarrels to chew over that they will turn on their marshals and give them a right hiding in their own way. Procedure again – I and I alone possess this key . . . here . . . which opens the bus door from inside and from outside. This key must carefully remain in my keeping all the time. At all times I shall be in the vicinity of the bus should you urgently require me. This door will not open from either side without my key here. And I want you to remember when you get out there, you will see nothing but an almighty wall of blackish brownish faces of a darker hue etcetera (no offence meant, Constable). And I want you to bear in mind a historical fact. It has taken three hundred years to ship out over twelve million of *them* from their native Africa. It appears that *now*, owing to the blatant slackness of our immigration laws, entirely due to Labour Party bungling

37

I might say, it appears as if there is a world conspiracy to bring all that twelve million and more back into our happy community, as if by right. Nevertheless, this carnival today will not be a riotous and joyful occasion until every last manjack there has gone home. Cup of tea anyone?

[BEV *produces her tea flask and a plastic beaker. Pours. Just for a few seconds it is more noticeable just how close the floats and bands are to the bus. Just long enough for* DRISS *to have a sip of his cuppa.*]

DRISS: . . . All right, boys and girls . . . let's get ourselves organized. Mufti inspection and full kit examination. No dragging the feet.

[*The* GIRLS *go back behind the curtain. They, if possible, can conceal themselves from the audience behind the second curtain they have rigged up.*

The BOYS *commence opening their cumbersome sacks.*

DOUG *and* FIRESTONE *sit side by side waiting.* FIRESTONE *has little to do but put on a black tie and button his shirt.*]

[*to the boys*] I want to be absolutely convinced by you young herberts that you have packed your equipment properly and I do not want to hear of you returning to your camps with any of it missing. This is expensive modern toggings which has been supplied to us courtesy of the Commission of the European Police Communities in order that we may exchange notes on said effectiveness of toggings. All this rubbish is ex-patent rubbish. And it is the intention of the nine member country police departments to rationalize these toggings to a single uniform under the terms of the EEC original charter of free exchange of ideas. Now what has Father Christmas from Brussels sent you lucky lads?

[GARY *and* KEVIN *and* DARRYL *dip into the sacks. Each item they fetch out is the parallel item to avoid any confusion. The first item is a four-foot length of polished hardwood. A label is attached with the appropriate wording.*]

DRISS: Four-foot length of polished hardwood – a truncheon.
GARY [*reading*]: Anti-pobelhaufe knuttel it says here, sir.
DRISS: Anti-pobelhaufe means anti-*them* outside.

[*The* BOYS *place the items carefully. Next they fetch out an unusual-looking helmet with hideous goggle holes of perspex. A strip of airtight sealer at the neckline is for eventual tamping on to the overall's top.*]

A gas-proof helmet. And a pair of anti-toxic mittens.

KEVIN: I've got two left hands, sir.

DRISS: Who's perfect, private?

GARY [*reading*]: A panzer schutz gasanzeiger verdecken.

[*The* BOYS *haul out a silver one-piece overall which possesses very ungainly boxing-glove mittens with little room for finger or wrist movement. The overall is zipped up from the back. The front crutch area is a negotiable flap.*]

DRISS: A light duty weight inflammable silver overall said to be resistant to atomic dust particles.

DARRYL [*reading*]: Me – feuergefahrlich uberzieihhose.

[*The* BOYS *pull out a stiff corset affair. It is made of padded material and has a matronly air about it.*]

DRISS: Your EEC bullet-proof bodice, right?

GARY [*reading*]: Me kugelfest korsett!

[*And follows a pair of cricket-like pads in each sack.*]

DARRYL: It's me – gamaschenscutsbekleidung! Leggins, sir.

[*It is noted that quiet* KEVIN *has started to make a little collection of the labels. The* BOYS *next fetch out a curved dark perspex shield each.*]

GARY [*reading*]: Eine schutzdach, sir.

[*And next a string of CS gas canisters on cartridge belts.*]

DARRYL: Me gaspatronengurt, sir.

DRISS: A for all found. Now what are we going to do with all this?

KEVIN [*flicking through his collection of labels*]: I'm dressin' up in them . . . an' goin' outside in 'em . . . in me panzer schutz gasanzeiger feuergefahrlich uberzieihhose not forgettin' me kugelfest korsett . . . an' . . . I'm goin' to wave around me anti-pobelhaufe knuttel here . . . an' give the first right cheeky mouth noodle a towsing round his obergrumpenfuhrerfatbumfartzl!

DRISS: Permission to undress, boys.

[*Although they are already half in and half out of their*

*khaki clothes, they commence a loose strip down to pants
and shirt.* DRISS *angles for* FIRESTONE *and* DOUG *and
they help to lace the inner pieces on to the* BOYS: *the
bodices and the leggings. It is clear that these inner garments
constrain their movements no end.*

Perhaps it is best that FIRESTONE *does not help* GARY *for
instance, but another. Once the bodices and leggings are on,
the* YOUTHS *begin to look ludicrous: kind of Widow
Twanky midriffs and US Football legs.*

*In any event it is a good moment to indicate the nearness
now of the floats and bands. The music is all Carnival a go,
laughter and the warmth and the pleasure of the outside
becomes clear to us.*

*The entire overall is large enough to encase all the inner
garments. Each lad is zipped up from the back to complete
the almost lunar metaphor. The gloved thick extremities of
the arms preclude all proper hand movement. They are thick
mitts for clasping truncheons and brandishing a shield.*

*Each flap possesses a zipper at the crutch. But clearly it is
not negotiable by the possessor of the need to go.*

Belts attached. GARY *and* DARRYL *and* KEVIN *look
glumly upon themselves.*

DRISS takes a helmet and places it on DARRYL's *head. He
fastens the seals round the neckline.*]

DRISS: . . . Two paces, Corporal?

[*Which* DARRYL *takes.* DRISS *hands him his truncheon
and shield.*]

. . . Come at me, Corporal?

[DARRYL *does so.* DRISS *trips him over with his foot.*
DARRYL *slips. Loses his balance. Topples on his back. It is
perfectly clear that once on his back with all that toggings*
DARRYL *cannot get up.* DARRYL *lies there waving his arms
and feet in the air, tortoise-like and shouts out from inside
his mask.*]

What does this teach us, then?

GARY: Sir, Lance Corporal Henshall is unable to get to his
feet after he has been knocked over in a horizontal position
on his back as it were.

DRISS: Correct.

[DARRYL *waves his arms and legs and hollers.*]

Nor can any of you do better.

[DRISS *and* FIRESTONE *help* DARRYL *to his feet.* DARRYL *stands there whilst* DRISS *shoves a helmet at each of the other* TWO LADS.]

Problem being P for paramount, you make it your solemn bounded Godly business not to be knocked over. Understood?

DARRYL/KEVIN/GARY: Sir!

DRISS: As we understand the conventions of the German and French para-military units, as soon as you are knocked down you do not move from that position. You call out in normal terms of distress and a fellow member of your support team will render you vertical again. On no account do you lean over to try to lift your fallen friend, on account of the fact you yourself as like as not will fall over with him. Thus ensuring the pair of you out of action. We have, though, after certain testings, come up with an alternative measure should the going get very choppy. We will suppose for the sake of argument, that the Corporal here has indeed fallen over.

[*He pushes* DARRYL *with his hand and* DARRYL *once more goes on his back with his arms and legs waving.* DRISS *tamps on the helmets.*]

. . . So . . . what we advise, following testings, is this. It appears that the enemy has penetrated your defences and groups of three of you, of three or more, are lying down on the ground unable to call for back-up strength. In such case it is advisable that two of you assist the third of you to get to his feet and move off in search of back-up forces. And this is how we do it . . . roll over.

[FIRESTONE *and* DOUG *and* DRISS *help lay* KEVIN *and* GARY *in a prone pile on the floor.*]

. . . The two of you squeeze beneath the Corporal and slowly pressure him upwards in a lever-like process.

[GARY *and* KEVIN *roll beneath* DARRYL *and start to lever him up.*]

... The Corporal keeps as straight as he can, so that he is not a sagging burden on you two lads.

[GARY *and* KEVIN *lever him up by shoulder and by hand from the ground. Lowering their hands down his legs as* DARRYL *reaches a near vertical position. As he reaches this vertical position* ...]

... That's right ... as the Corporal reaches this vertical position he keeps his entire body weight stiffened, and, in due course, he can settle firmly on the flats of his feet, and the operation rescue is carried out to the satisfaction capital S for satisfaction of all, mission rescue accomplished.

[*As* DARRYL *reaches the vertical position stiff as a poker and upright, it transpires that* KEVIN *and* GARY *have pushed too far from behind and, of course,* DARRYL *falls flat on his face in the other direction, stiff as a poker, with a wallop.*

DRISS *and* FIRESTONE *and* DOUG *help all three lads up.*]

... On second thoughts, Corporal, perhaps you ought to just lie still and pray.

[*They take the helmets off the* LADS. *The* LADS *look very hot.*

The THREE GIRLS *come out from behind their rug curtain and walk on through the divider curtain down the aisle. There is a complete transformation.* BEV *is fully equipped in her lurid punk outfit. Bizarre make-up and garish colours.* ALICE *is well equipped in rather ordinary tourist-type clothes. It would be difficult to pin her down as anyone really, let alone a so-called tourist. But she is attractive and she waves her large and obvious handbag. As for* RAINE *— she is shaven-haired now, with a simple orange gown and sandals, her bell around her neck, and an impenetrable stare.* DRISS *and the* OTHERS *take in the sight.*]

BEV [*pause*]: ... Close your mouth, Darryl.

DRISS: Now — conduct. Any one of you at any given moment could be fair game for the Trots out there, the assorted wankers out there, the university educated too-clevers out there; to begin with doos and don'ts. If you are caught with an illegal lead-filled SPG cosh, remember it belongs to your dear old granny's lavatory chain which you have promised to mend. Before you smash any Marxist-Leninist student from New Zealand, first politely inquire as to the thickness of his back skull. Do not waste energy beating Asians. Their turbans contain Post Office savings books, paperback Korans and specially-stiffened pappadum curry sandwiches; plus up to forty yards of closely rolled anti-police material. Your arm'll fall off. Avoid striking the elderly and infirm, the handicapped and the blind, anybody in a wheelchair or wearing plaster of Paris neck supports. At the last resort, if a cripple raises his crutch at you in a manner thought threatening you may retaliate, but do not make the mistake of breaking the actual crutch, because sure as eggs it will be used later as evidence of brutality. At the worst, crack a skull but don't knock a wheel off of a wheelchair, right? Do not get involved in any fight unless you are certain of the presence of a fellow officer who can act as witness. You will find the TV cameras and itinerant artistic film makers will more likely be harnessed to tops of cars. Give them nothing to film, and give them no opportunity to catch you in an offensive role. If anything, make sure you are retreating from pressure of superior opposite numbers. And, if by dint of bad luck, a camera has focused on you at the moment of clubbing some silly fart to the floor, instantly pick the fart up and shake him in a manner not un-adjacent to silly bugger friendliness. And try your best restraint not to refer to a black American visitor with whom you are having an altercation as a shit-arsed golliwog the moment a BBC roving microphone is shoved under your nose. It is crucial you do not chase any of them down side-streets. You will find that each juncture, no matter how small, does have its duty officer. His job is to reinforce the one road of passage given to *them*, and he does not want to be derailed from this position. Pick up all young white children you might find who have been bowled over by the crush. Make no attempt whatsoever to pick up or aid a black kid, you will immediately be mistaken for police brutality against harmless minors. Pregnant women suffering from the heat, loonies, whites in particular, who suffer sudden St Vitus' Dance symptoms and start threshing about, and Japanese tourists who appear to have lost their way back to the Kensington Hilton – all three groups are more trouble than they are worth.

[*To* ALICE]

. . . One of the commonest arguments we heard last year thrown at us after the carnival was the one about more arrests being made in the Cup Final than the entire carnival of half a million *them*. It is to be hoped this year that we can disprove this sly innuendo that the police are not doing enough to enforce the law. Anti-riot costs are mounting. It is up to us to ensure that a million pounds of the tax-payers' money is not being wasted.

[*He opens her bag and takes out a camera with a shoulder leash. He puts the leash on* ALICE's *shoulder. And leaves the bag half-clasped, not fully closed. He alters* ALICE's *neckline and undoes the top button.*]

. . . The secret of your success is to keep the bag just loosened enough at the catch to attract the eye. And be prepared at all times for him to snatch the camera strap hard. Do not let the strap cut your arm. In any event the strap should be weak enough to break. I . . .

RAINE: Sir?

DRISS: I'd be a lot happier if . . .

RAINE: What, sir?

DRISS: Sergeant Hollinsloe, it still strikes me we are not making the maximum use of our target policy. After all, it is a warm day, the sun is shining, it is the day of the carnival and I would like to see this officer at her most inviting.

RAINE: I don't understand. Is there something wrong with Alice's outfit?

DRISS: She's wearing a bra. If I may say so . . . it is extremely unusual for a modern girl to go around with a thick white chastity belt around her bosoms, particularly in a parade like this outside.

RAINE: Is it the type of bra she wears which you don't like?

DRISS: If a thief can clearly make out the shape of her

nipples, the officer's chances of success are very much more increased.

RAINE: Alice?

ALICE: As I told you before I am prone to these rashes, sir.

RAINE: If it is absolutely necessary I can lend you some cream.

ALICE [*to* RAINE]: Sarge, I don't want the cream to get all over my –

RAINE: Alice?

ALICE: Sarge?

RAINE [*a little reprovingly*]: Alice.

> [ALICE *hesitates. Then she boils over inside her. She reaches inside her shirt and yanks away a front-fastening strapless bra. Angry and blushing she one-twos smartly in front of* DRISS.]

ALICE [*to* DRISS]: . . . Nipples, sir!

> [DRISS *turns away.*]

DRISS: . . . Where was I, man?

DOUG [*a little confused*]: Clothing, sir?

DRISS: Correct. Clothes and disguise. *Them* out there have something called Black Mas. We in here have adopted something I like to call White Mas. The art of adopting disguise. The art of assuming the role of a common hero to our side. As against their side. On our team as it were we have the punk . . .

> [*At* BEV.]

. . . a punk is not, in our understanding, an example of social revolt. If anything it is merely a symptom of resentment directed at numerous pop-stars who have deserted this country to avoid their tax obligations. Essentially, the punk is allied with unemployment and the status of the new under-class as it is called. So, these assorted safety pins are, in the opinion of Combined Operations HQ, more a desire to pin together the remnants of the status quo, than to reject it altogether. Punks are friendly.

> [*To* RAINE.]

. . . The Hari Krishna youths who dance up and down Oxford Street, who worship Krishna, brave and fearless Hindu boy God. They are, essentially, apolitical and have no interest in disturbing the status quo. The Hari Krishnas are on our side.

[*He glances at* DOUG.]

. . . Combined Ops have valued for years the grimy emaciated hippy who can infiltrate all drug racketeering with the exception of the Chinese Dragon Mafia, and the Rastafarian Ganga weed sellers. Curiously, after emerging with a howl of protest in the 1960s, the hippy opted for drugs and eastern mumbo-jumbo and allowed his political conscience to slide into isolationist life-styles. If anything, Combined Operations is convinced the leftover hippy grown old is the natural son of a hierarchic system of values. The hippy is no traitor to the status quo. On our side, out there, Special Branch men are disguised as one-legged RAF fighter pilots, and impoverished Rhodesian farmers reduced to playing violins in the London underground. And the Army has a ten-year-old horse trained to a Redbrick-university standard which can lie down and feign dead when a bovver-boy-lefty kicks it . . . now where was I?

GARY: Woman Police Constable Alice's nipples, sir?

KEVIN: Lay off, Simpkin.

DRISS: Mas . . . That's where I was, Black Mas. What is Mas? And what are Mas workshops? You will have noticed over the years how the black communities put up on their floats their so-called 'Figures representing the Forces of Victory'. Well, a Mas workshop is where they design the costumes for these archetypal heroes. And what an affront they are to any kind of civilized intelligence. Do you know what you will see on this parade? You will see airmen dummies on a float – these are Cuban paratroopers flown into Mozambique and Angola. You will see terrorist dummies holding up papier-mâché machine guns – these are so-called members of the Patriotic Front who defeated the internal white regime of Rhodesia. You will see black girls in orange and green drum majorette suits – these are to be interpreted as freedom fighters from the Caribbean islands as yet unyoked from the Queen's Commonwealth of

Nations. There will be banners with the names of 'Che' and 'Toussant L'Ouverture' and 'Moisé'. Black dictators from the other side of the world. There will be on a float, for certain, the image of a piccaninny dangling from a gibbet. This is to be treated as a reference to the Queen's decision to hang the scoundrel Michael X. You might come across the figure of a bound and bloodied boy in a chicken coop – it will be a metaphor for the death of a South African escapee called Biko. You might observe on a float a dozen or so men in prison stripes in a corner of a cell. This is an allusion to the outrageous lie that twelve black prisoners have died inside British jails in the past five years. And from time to time, on the coats of dangerous twistle-haired freaks called Rastafarians you will see black star badges. A black star badge is the symbol of the notorious criminal racketeer Marcus Garvey, from Jamaica, who once ordained a fleet of ships entitled The Black Star Shipping Line Company Limited should ship back the world's entire black population to their true Zion homeland of Africa. [*Shaking his head. A weariness.*] . . . Sometimes dear Lord . . . I ask myself . . . are we all *au fait*? . . . good lads. . . . They have, you see, their Mas workshop. *Them* do out there. I'm proud to say that we have our own Mas camp of heroes right here.

[*He looks around at all of them. An eerie calm.*

For a moment DRISS *appears to falter. A tiredness. The nerve breaking. A hesitant yawing of the sensibilities as if drunk with the scene.*]

DRISS: . . . In this bus . . . here . . . don't we? . . . Sergeant? Detective Sergeant?

DOUG: Mas, sir. The art of Mas.

[*The music outside has come to a sudden halt. Although it has been loud enough to speak over it has never approached overlap on the speeches. Always background. But always coming closer. Suddenly the silence outside is uncanny.* DRISS *looks up and waits. Not a sound for the moment. As if the entire carnival has come to a halt around the corner.*]

CRACKLE VOICE: This is Partic Thistle here. Come in Charley Tango Bravo.

DRISS: . . . Charley Tango Bravo here . . . Come in Partic Thistle . . . over.

CRACKLE VOICE: Hallo Charley Tango Bravo . . . This is an announcement. We have stopped the bands at Cambridge Gardens junction with St Lawrence Terrace. We have advised them of the impracticality of proceeding on to the corner of Acklam Road without proper police escort. Once the floats start up again, they will turn this corner and be with you in less than four minutes. We must provide maximum escort power at your junction. As soon as the music strikes up, and we let the people pass, you have the baton in your hand. Over and out Charley Tango Bravo.

DRISS: Of course. Right!

[DRISS *and* FIRESTONE *put the helmets back on the* LADS *and tamp the airtight flaps from the neck rings. They give the* LADS *their shields and their truncheons.*]

DRISS: Now let's see. Girls?

GARY: Excuse me.

DRISS: Last chance to attend the L for lavatory. Quick chop.

GARY: Excuse me, sir, that's what I'm saying, sir.

DRISS: Who is this?

GARY: Private Gary Simpkin, sir. Caught short with a weak bladder, sir. Don't know how I done it, sir.

DRISS: Too late to undress you, boy. It's a difficult enough operation to keep you upstanding on your two front feet, boy. Constable, lend a hand.

FIRESTONE: Come along.

[FIRESTONE *unzips the little ticker zip at* GARY's *crutch.* GARY *leaps. Clearly he cannot service himself with those gloves.*]

GARY: You bloody won't!

DRISS: He bloody will! Or you pour it in your boots. That's an order.

[FIRESTONE *guides* GARY *through the curtain to the end of the bus.* FIRESTONE *stands behind* GARY *and pushes him into the closet.* GARY *is so wide he can hardly fit. It is a*

48

squeeze. FIRESTONE *puts his hand around* GARY's *waist and helps him.*]

GARY: Bloody nerve! ... bloody cheek! ... gerr off! ... ow Christ! ... Humilibloodyation ... !

[*Whilst* GARY *finishes and* FIRESTONE *zips him back up and leads him into the front section again.* DRISS *picks up the two/way.*]

RADIO: Come in Charley Tango Bravo.

DRISS: ... Charley Tango Bravo to Partic Thistle? ... Come in please?

CRACKLE VOICE: Stand by Charley Tango Bravo. . . Partic Thistle here...stand by ready...OK for GO. Over and out.

DRISS: Stand by.

[DRISS *puts the two/way down. All of them,* BEV *and* ALICE *and* RAINE, DOUG *and* FIRESTONE, GARY *and* DARRYL *and* KEVIN, *and* DRISS *too, take up waiting positions in a line approaching the one exit door.* DRISS *closest with his key.*

The GIRLS *change positions. The* BOYS *too. Then* BEV *is beside* DARRYL *and* ALICE *beside* KEVIN *and* RAINE *beside* GARY. FIRESTONE *and* DOUG *together.*

They sink back against the bench seats and some sit down. The LADS *can only stand erect.*

The sense of anticipation.

They become very lowered. A depression settles in.

They are at their most vulnerable. A dulled quality.]

DOUG [*very low voice*]: ... Why did you join, Firestone? Eh?

FIRESTONE [*quiet and flat*]: ... There was nothing else.

DOUG: Just the money?

FIRESTONE: That's all, that's all. Can you think of any other reason?

[DOUG *shakes his head.*]

... Nor me, man.

[DRISS *is poised waiting.*

It is something in their voices, a muted quality like the step into a stone chapel out of the bright sunlight.]

BEV: ... All right are you, Darryl?

DARRYL: ... Yearh ... all right.

49

RAINE: .... All right, girls?
  [*The* GIRLS *nod and lean against the side of the bus.*]
DARRYL [*softly to* BEV]: Gary and Kevin are going to Belfast in January.
ALICE [*to* KEVIN]: ... That true?
KEVIN [*nodding*]: Darryl's already been and done his four months there.
ALICE [*to* KEVIN]: You don't want to go to Belfast ... do you?
  [*They lapse into silence.*
  DRISS *switches the seat lights out from a switch by the door.*]
DRISS [*quiet*]: ... Lights out now.
  [*In the dark.*]
RAINE: ... It is lovely outside now.
GARY: ... That's what they said on the weather.
RAINE: ... Makes it better, doesn't it?
GARY: ... Keeps the old pecker up.
RAINE: ... Nothing but sunshine out there all day.
  [*Comes a terrific start up of what sounds like a dozen floats simultaneously let loose in the air. It is the entire section of this parade which has been held back on the corner of a road less than forty yards away from the bus. Within moments the marchers and the kids and the floats and the bands and the spirit of the carnival grow into a crescendo around the bus. Nothing but shuffle and pummel of feet and shoulders outside. Free association of musical parade and peoples.*
  Moments more and the entire bus starts to wobble. The pressure from the crowd seems to want to shake the bus down to its chassis.
  Those inside the bus hold on to anything they can for support. The bus appears to be moving almost in the crush.
  DRISS *unlocks the door with his special key, and one by one bundles all of them out into the flickering white sunlight and the shock of faces and shoulders; a sea of people out there.*]
DRISS [*over the music*]: ... Let's 'ave ya! OK for go!
  [*Out they tumble into the crowd.*
  The carnival bands and the crowds swell with a roar. The carnival music continues at a pitch as the bus door closes behind them.]

ACT TWO

*Once the audience is back seated the music of the floats can begin
to fade away. This time the floats are heading up the road in the
opposite direction from the commencement of the music location
in the beginning of Act One. It is important to indicate through
the music that the floats and instruments are leaving the area of
the bus and heading up towards Kensington.*

[*The door opens and* DRISS *leads in* DOUG. DRISS *helps*
DOUG *up the steps.* DOUG *is a bit winded. He looks a trifle
out of step with his clothing for he has lost his wig. His own
natural hair is very short and sharply clipped.*

DRISS *helps* DOUG *to a seat.* DRISS *carefully shuts the
door.*]

DRISS: . . . Good lad . . . catch a haircut did you on the
way? . . .

DOUG [*winded*]: I lost my partner, I decided to go it alone.

DRISS: Nothing broken?

DOUG [*breathing deep for air*]: . . . Excuse me, sir! . . . You
know, I was actually that close and I blew it!

DRISS: Lost a nail, did you?

DOUG: I'd been following this guy . . . and he was finally
coming round . . . I said I had no money at all and sod it,
it was carnival, wasn't it? . . . working him round that way
. . . and he was going for it . . . the story . . . in a corner of
the Electric Cinema emergency door he stops . . . a mo . . .
I didn't see this amateur flatfoot behind me . . . and this
black guy's pulling a transparent plastic bag of Thai Grass
big enough . . . enough grass in it to feed Red Rum his
bloody elevenses there was . . . and this flatfoot from somewhere comes up behind me and taps me on my shoulder.
And the black head sees the constable quick. Pushes the
whole bag into me arms, panics, and belts off into a sea of
black heads comin' round the corner. I'm left standing
there, ain' I? Like Father Pusher Christmas I am. Holding

the bag I am. And the flatfoot who's just jumped out of his panda car says something like 'What's this, son, then? Dry preserve sea-weed is it!' An' I was swearing at him and telling him I'd have his guts – he'd only bloody lumbered me just at the moment of clobbering a pusher with a possession-with-intent-to-supply. I actually had the bastard in the palm of me hand and I was about to do him! This idiot copper's got me by the ear tellin' me his anything-you-have-to-say-in-defence rubbish. And I'm tellin' him for Christ's sake I'm Special Patrol Group, Tulse Hill Station, aren't I? An' he's saying to me back 'I was in the girl guides before this lot, son.' I'm a Detective Sergeant. I'm S P G you nana so lay off me! He said 'That's right, son, and I've heard April ducks fart in church on Sundays, too!' [*Catching his breath.*] . . . whoooor . . . I was that angry I kneed him one. And he grabbed me hair and pulled. So I had a choice. Go back to Ladbroke Grove Cottage and spend the night explaining it an' asking for me long hairs back or piss off smartish.

DRISS: Very hard cheese that one . . .

DOUG: I could have killed that copper. What do we bother for? Putting our head on the block? Whole place is bloody leaking with uniformed amateurs, who, once they get behind the wheel of a Ford Cortina panda car it's a seventy mile an hour ego wank all the way home. Why do we bother?

DRISS: . . . I bother.

DOUG: If he had took me to the station, and arrested me and charged me I'd have been fucked. Have you any idea, sir, how difficult it is to get your monicker off the Police National Computer once you've been arrested in the street? Bloody murder it is I'm sayin'. I have to apply to my Chief under terms governed by National Security Classification. He has to go along cap in hand to C. Eleven Department and beg their Criminal Intelligence Collection to strike out everything down to my left lumbar region beauty mole. So you tell me, sir, why we bother?

DRISS: I came out of the 'emergency' in Brunei in 1952, after

twenty silly arse months in Spencer Chapman's army
chasing a terr called Chin Peng. I'd had enough. I met this
girl whose father was general manager for Raleigh Bicycles,
Singapore. Married her in the second floor bar of old
Raffles Hotel. I'd had enough. We had a son and she went
back to teaching kids history. My wife used to say the tide's
against us. It was like trying to innoculate these kids
against communism with a couple of jabs of anti-distemper
vaccine. Before my wife died, she used to say to me there is
no such thing as moral certainty any more. All there is –
just an unending reassertion of social truths. The cracks are
in the paving stones and all we can do is patch them from
time to time with Araldite. After Lee Kuan declared a
Republic I came back to the UK with the boy. I tried my
hand at breeding Bedlington terriers. Lovely little rare
breed, and a goer, mind you, a goer. Can course the ears
off a lurcher. When my son died I packed it in. Nigh bank-
rupt I was, too, with private medical bills. Come back into
the army double quick pronto. [*Pause.*] . . . One of these
days if you prompt me I'll tell you just how my wife and
the boy died. [*Pause.*] . . . Not much of a market these days
for breeding champion white Bedlington terriers, you
know. [*Pause.*] . . . B for bother, I bother.

> [*There is a sudden banging outside the door. And* DRISS
> *fetches out his master key to open the inside lock to let in the
> girls –* ALICE *looks rather soiled and untidy.* BEV *and*
> RAINE *follow seemingly quite relieved to be back.*
>
> DOUG *takes himself off behind the first aisle curtain to
> change from his hippy toggings to things he has brought in a
> small bag.*
>
> ALICE *is worn out and throws herself across the bench seat.*]

BEV: . . . Home sweet home . . . it is!

DRISS: Well done, girls . . . nothing damaged?

ALICE [*getting her breath back*]: God almighty it is rough out
there. I thought I was going to die for lack of oxygen. And
hot! Blimey it is! Then I waited until the largest bands on
those floats had gone by. I just can't stand that cha cha cha
calypso thing, it drives me out in nervous spots. Waited

until the dancing girls had gone. And the lads, you know the real likely ones, were coming along behind in groups. Absolutely asking for it. Just hanging around the shop-fronts looking and waiting. Desperate to show off like. Far as I was concerned I thought . . . come into . . . my parlour little fly . . . suddenly . . . I swung my camera and the bag in a pretty open manner . . . you should have seen the idiot take the bait! . . . like a lemming over a cliff . . . one came either side of me. I made sure I knew where the police car was waiting. The first one wrenched so hard on the camera strap it burned, it actually made a burn mark on my shoulder. And at that moment the other one grabbed the handbag. He tried to put his hand inside it. Because he could see the catch half-open – changed his mind and just grabbed. I blew the whistle and fell over. While I was still over he couldn't get the bag off me without turning me over. I dropped it, and jumped up and ran so hard after the camera idiot. I was dead lucky he was going in the correct direction. Right towards the panda off the corner which he couldn't see. Six of them got out the car and fell on him. Blood all over his mouth, an arm broken and he was screaming about his ribs. When I got there he was saying I was his girl-friend and he'd gone off with the camera to catch a snap of the last float. I was his girl-friend! I said I should cocoa I said! . . . I've never run so hard . . .

DRISS: Well done, my dear . . . Sergeant?

RAINE: I felt completely naked the moment I stepped out there. I had to break clear of the crowd. Wham, without realizing I had walked straight into a group of real Hari Krishnas on the corner of Blenheim Crescent. I almost had a fit. They grabbed me tight and told me not to move an inch away from them otherwise we'd get lost. I've got no choice then but stay put. And in no time, when the leader found a clear run down the street he had us dingle-dangling our bells, shuffling like this . . . from side to side . . . Hari Hari Krishna! I couldn't escape. We were in the open on Kensington Park Gardens, who should I see but this bloody horrible Special Branch lad I met once before. He

came up – there am I – dingle-dangle Hari Krishna! ...
'I know you. You were a WRAC. Sgt. Hollinsloe isn't it?'
Jumped up Criminal Intelligence copper snuk his way into
the SB. I never fancied him. I said – I've seen the light. It's
a new me. I'm in free love, drugs and incest, seven-day
fasts, prayers on mats, giving my all to poverty, sackcloth
and Hindu Gods, and all Special Branch agents are fag-end
human beings! You should have seen his face fall off!

BEV [*holding up one of her Nazi daggers*]: I got two for offensive weapons. I tried to buy one off him. And he was about
to take the money when the squad car jumped on him.
Cinch really. Then I got depressed and went for a walk. I'd
rather it had been a white youth really. These black boys
don't know who Adolf Hitler is, you know. And I was
trying to avoid a right bunch of black drape teds who
wanted to chase me. I ask you – who in his right mind
wants to run in poor old teddy boys. You get laughed out
of court. They never carry amphetamines even. And this
amazing-looking punk comes up. White and vermilion
hair in stripes and incredible green-coloured natural eyes.
Mind you only about two foot tall he was. 'Hallo you fat
cow!' he said, 'My name's Ian Brady. What's yourn –
Myra?' He said 'Want a Unigate pint bottle thrust all the
way up?' 'No', I said, 'and looking down at you I doubt if
you could go to a Japanese fibre-tip pen top.' He loved that.
He said 'I really like you, cow.' An' thspoorh! Spat all in
me face. I said and I love you, too, an' thspoorh back in his.
And it was thspoorh! And thspoorh! Spray all over both of
us. Thspoorh! And he said 'Look 'ere, cow-hole, if yerve got
the money, I'll take you to the Ian Dury fing by Camden
Town unnergroun' tonight. An' after, we'll get the 62B
bus, an' yer can toss me orf stoopid in the back row seat
while I get yer tits arht.' I hesitated ... then I thought to
myself – is there no end to true romance?

[DRISS *goes to the door, there is a hammering and an
urgency from the crowds outside. In near distance the music
is still going away.* DRISS *opens the door with his special key
and hauls in the three lads. They all possess their helmets*

55

and their truncheons and their shields. DRISS *carefully pushes the door back. He has difficulty in edging people out so that he can shut it. At last they are all safe again.*

The GIRLS *help the lads who are sat slowly but bolt upright on the bench seat together Their helmets are taken off. And they breathe heavily.*

Perspiration drips from them. The exhaustion is clear to see.]

DRISS: ... At ease, lads ...

DARRYL [*weakly*]: Oh ... at ease, sir ...

DRISS: Rendezvous O K with the other soldiers, did you?

DARRYL [*breathless, knackered*]: We ... joined up with the other armoured groups ... all in a line ... cut off hundreds of them between Elgin Avenue and ... where?

GARY [*head back, exhausted*]: Elgin Crescent ... and ... Colville Gardens ...

DARRYL? Then ... when they saw us in line ... you should have seen their faces ...

DRISS: Terrified, were they?

DARRYL: No, sir ... not ... they just became angry, fantastically angry ... running all over ... trying to climb iron railings to get behind us ... just anger, sir.

DRISS: You had back-up?

DARRYL: Had a ... wall of policemen behind us. They kept shouting at us to let the kids get behind us so's they be trapped in the middle.

GARY: Click clunk bricks came over. Big as your two feet. They thought we were going to use the canisters on them. They kept shouting *gas*!

DARRYL: Our presence ... gets them so angry, you know. But it takes the sting out of the police work. They can wait until they've got the ones they want in a corner.

[*Out from behind the curtain steps* DOUG *with his hippy gear in his small bag. He is a new man. Crisp clean face. Short back and brushed. Red complexion. Shined boots and crisp shirt and nice trousers. Mum's boy. The lads do not recognize him.*]

DOUG: Permission to leave, sir?

DRISS: I'll let you out.

DOUG: Trra lads! Trra girls!

DRISS: Nice meeting you . . . keep it up . . .

DOUG: Nice meeting you, sir.

DRISS: One of these days we'll meet up. And I'll tell you that story. How me wife and me boy died on me.

[DRISS *lets* DOUG *out. A half-salute to* DRISS. DRISS *closes the door. A sudden blast of voices and crowded street enters the bus. Shuffle and congress. The Doppler effect of the music.*]

GARY [*after* DOUG]: . . . Who was that then?

DARRYL [*shrugs*]: Who was that, Bev?

BEV [*tweaks his nose*]: Ooh . . . you right thicky you are!

DRISS [*to lads*]: Let's 'ave yer then, boys! Canisters all found are they?

[*He inspects their cartridge belts.*]

DARRYL: All intact, sir!

GARY: All intact, sir!

KEVIN: All intact, sir!

[DRISS *checks. Because it is difficult for the boys to look down at their own waistline.*]

DRISS: . . . All found.

GARY: God . . . sir . . . if we'd tossed canisters, they would have come for us wiv everyfing. They were so angry when they saw the cans.

DRISS: Not so much that, lad. You toss a canister at *them*, and one of them has got the guts to toss it back to you, you're in no end of trouble. Last thing your police back-up need is a noseful of CS gas whilst trying to maintain mob control. So, when you pack proper tonight, double-check all cans. Not one to be missing. Understood?

BOYS: Sir!

DRISS: Of course, I was more worried about sky-thieving pickpockets out there. The street is stiff with pickpockets out there. If you'd have lost a canister to one of them, I'd get the shit, wouldn't I? . . . Dismiss . . .

[DRISS *finds his key to let himself out with. He turns by the door and holds up key.*]

Sergeant, I'm stationing myself outside the door. I don't know where that constable's taken himself off to. I'll wait

57

there for him. Just remember, I have the only key in or out of this bus, and if you hear me shout for help I'll spring the door fast – and we may need your help. Understood?

RAINE: Sir!

[DRISS *lets himself out. Shuts the door behind him. The boys and girls relax for a five-second pause.*

Then there is banging outside the door. The unmistakable feel of a punch-up and a crowd growing right outside the door. DRISS's *voice shouts out.*]

DRISS'S VOICE: . . . Give a hand!

[*The bus door swings open.* DRISS *is pulling a person. He steps up into the bus. Then steps out again as if to push the person up.*

DARRYL *and* BEV *run to help. They each grab an arm of* FIRESTONE's. *He has lost his jacket and his helmet. His blue police shirt and tie are torn about.* DRISS *is somewhere below trying to push* FIRESTONE *on up. Others below outside in the street are trying to pull* FIRESTONE *back.*

It is a tug of war. GARY *and* RAINE *hang on to* DARRYL *and* BEV *too.*]

GARY: He's ours! Not theirs!

[*They lose.* FIRESTONE *is being dragged back out. They cannot hold him.* DARRYL *and* BEV *topple and let go.*

Shouts of triumph from outside.

DARRYL *and* GARY *manage to slam the door shut on the outside.*]

RAINE: . . . They think Firestone belongs to them!

GARY: Just because he's black, it don't mean he is black.

[*More hammering outside.* KEVIN *looking a bit winded and rigid. Then shouts and heaving sounds.*

A hand begins to desperately scrub off some of the whiting on the outside window. DRISS's *hair and eye-line appear. He must be hanging on to something a couple of feet above his normal height.*]

DRISS [*other side of glass*]: . . . boys! . . . I'm locked out! My God, my key! Some bastard's just picked my pocket!!!

[DRISS *disappears under a welter of shouts and abuse. He has slipped down to the ground out of sight.*

Up the hill towards Kensington the float bands produce an

unusual exuberance. The buoyant calypso has a renewed
pleasure in it. A carnival delight for the heroes of victory.
GARY *glances at* KEVIN. *Detects the strangeness building*
there.
But all their attention is concentrated on the outside. The
voices and the hammering there. And gradually the bus
begins to rock. To and fro to and fro at us and away from
us as if twenty pairs of hands are rocking it off its wheels.
The rhythm increases.
DARRYL *leans heavily against the back wall. The back*
wall which is nearest to them outside. He leans with all his
weight. The others follow suit. Except KEVIN *who hesitates.*
A volcano in his mind begins.]

DARRYL: They're trying to push the bus over! . . . lean! . . .
put your weight! . . . they want to rock it over that way!

[*He points to our near side of the bus. They all lean with all*
their might. Then KEVIN *decides to join them.*]

KEVIN: . . . Oh God Christ! . . . lean! . . .

[*The rocking is so fierce that they are all thrown back and*
forth. The entire bus is about to go over. It is KEVIN *who*
takes a bad tumble on his side. He cannot get up easily. The
noise outside is intense. It is clear that DRISS *must be out of*
reach by now.
Gradually the rocking eases. Some of the voices depart. The
crowd seems to be moving on now.
As the bus settles again on its wheels they take stock.
KEVIN *is lying there. There is a hissing noise. He is on his*
side holding on to his canisters.
DARRYL *and* GARY *reach for him to help him.*
KEVIN *unhitches a spitting canister. It has a small crack*
in it. The spume is a thin spurt. But not immediately
dangerous.]

ALICE: . . . Kev?
KEVIN: . . . Look!
GARY: You split it!
KEVIN: . . . Jeesus!

[KEVIN *tosses it to* GARY.
GARY *tosses it over to* DARRYL.
DARRYL *drops it.*]

RAINE *catches it in time.*]

BEV [*opens slit window*]: . . . Here!

[DARRYL *stops* RAINE *tossing it out of the window. He pulls her hand back. They all cough. Eyes melt.*]

DARRYL: . . . No! . . . You'll start a bloody war!

[DARRYL *holds it up spitting and spuming.*]

. . . Cloth! . . . Plastic bag, first-aid kit . . . Anything! [*to* RAINE] . . . Shut that window!

[ALICE *fetches a woolly jumper. She gingerly wraps the canister. Then* BEV *finds a spare shirt. She too overwraps it.* GARY *brings something. Lungs aching. Streaming eyes.*]

KEVIN: . . . We can't keep it in here!

DARRYL [*wrapping the canister*]: Got to!

KEVIN: You can't leave it in here.

DARRYL: You heard what Driss said.

[ALICE *takes the wrapped spitting object from* DARRYL.]

ALICE: . . . I know . . . the toilet.

DARRYL: Not in there. There's chemicals in there!

[*She runs behind the aisle curtain and chooses a bench seat toward the back of the bus.* RAINE *and* KEVIN *follow her. She places the wrapped canister inside her own suitcase, shuts lid and locks it.*]

That's it, then.

KEVIN: [*agitated*]: Oh yes?

GARY: There's no way out.

RAINE: Driss'll come back.

KEVIN: Oh yes?

GARY [*tries door*]: He said – didn't he – only opens with the key!

[GARY *turns back and goes to the rear of the bus.* KEVIN *busily follows* GARY's *steps and tries the door. Hopeless.* KEVIN *pummels at it. Turns to follow* GARY *back.*]

. . . The emergency door is welded in, see.

[KEVIN *follows with abrupt movements. He tries the emergency back door. He studies the welding.*

GARY, *a second or two ahead of* KEVIN, *tries the closet. No go out there either.*]

'S'nothing 'ere – just a door to the bog.

[KEVIN *busy and frantic follows on behind, shoves* GARY *out of the way to see for himself.*]

KEVIN: ... Nothing in there ...

[KEVIN *looks after* GARY, KEVIN *studies his back as* GARY *walks away from him towards the front of the bus.* KEVIN *follows as if he is sure* GARY *will find a loophole.* GARY *leans over the driver's seat area.*]

GARY: ... It's impossible to get out ...

DARRYL: ... Or in without the key ...

KEVIN [*more to himself*]: ... or in without, right! ...

[*The boys and girls ease up.* DARRYL *and* GARY *are perspiring heavily. The girls help zip them out of their silver suitings. They are relieved the crowd has moved on. They are thankful to get out of the overalls. Beneath the overalls they have the pads and bodices buckled on to them still. Obscene appearance.*

They have hardly noticed KEVIN, *who has gone back to the main door – the first door* GARY *checked out.* KEVIN *has gone down on his knees and he is shaking and trying to squeeze himself into the door as if he wants to ooze his way through the crack in the door. He is shaking and losing control. But silently. The boys are too glad to just have the zips lifted and the suitings taken off to notice yet –*]

DARRYL: ... Oh relief! ...

[ALICE *notices* KEVIN. *The others follow suit.* ALICE *runs to him. She tries to pull him back. She cannot. He is too heavy. Still in his overall. Shaking and palsied and crushed against the door. The others pull him back and twist him into a position where they can loosen the zip and open the overall. His head going, his hands and feet floppy on them. Their worried expressions.*]

ALICE: ... Kev! ...

[*Now they sit him up. And some of the dopey slavering look has vanished.* RAINE *looks into his eyes. She lifts back the lower lids.*]

... Come on, Kev ... go on, Kev, you're all right.

DARRYL: Make him talk.

ALICE: ... Kev? ...

DARRYL: Make him read something. Anything.

[ALICE *finds* DRISS's *copy of the* Daily Telegraph *and reads advertisement on front page.*]

61

ALICE [*reading*]: ARE YOU LEGAL, DECENT, HONEST AND TRUTHFUL?

RAINE [*quick to cotton, out very loud*]: . . . ARE YOU LEGAL, DECENT, HONEST AND TRUTHFUL?

DARRYL/GARY: [*top of their voices, belting it*]: . . . ARE YOU LEGAL, DECENT, HONEST AND TRUTHFUL?

RAINE/BEV/DARRYL/GARY [*letting loose, raved release, gunning tongues*]: ARE YOU LEGAL, DECENT, HONEST AND TRUTHFUL?

KEVIN: . . . are you . . . are you . . .

ALICE: Right! . . . LEGAL, DECENT, HONEST AND TRUTHFUL.

KEVIN: . . . ARE YOU . . . LEGAL, LEGAL, LEGAL . . .

GARY: LEGAL, DECENT and fucking HONEST and TRUTHFUL!

KEVIN: [*got it, at last, belts it*]: ARE YOU LEGAL, DECENT, HONEST AND TRUTHFUL? ARE YOU LEGAL, DECENT, HONEST AND TRUTHFUL? ARE YOU . . .

ALICE [*gently seals his mouth with her hand*]: . . . That's it, Kev . . . all right, lovey? . . . all right now . . . sssh.

GARY: Yearh . . . that's it, Kev . . . don't make a long player out of it.

[ALICE *kisses* KEVIN's *face. Takes her hand from his mouth. Very gently and kindly kisses his cheeks.* KEVIN *slowly eases up. Breathes deeply. Begins to relax.* ALICE *holds him. A pause. A stillness.*]

DARRYL: . . . I told you Kevin was going to Belfast in January. [*They slump in seats and against the floor and the wall.* RAINE *is nearest a window.*]

GARY: . . . Hot, init? . . .

[ALICE *is taking more of* KEVIN's *padding off. He lets her turn him this way then that in the bench seat. She lays the pads and bodice on top of his bag.* KEVIN *lies along the bench seat.*]

KEVIN: . . . Could sleep a week on this . . . what's in it, Alice? [ALICE *pulls at a long zipper which stretches the front of the bench seat. She lifts a bit of the flap. And feels inside.*]

ALICE: . . . Foam rubber, mate . . . top quality.

KEVIN: . . . Nothin' but the best for me . . . eh?

[*She sits on the edge of the seat and strokes his hair back. Hair is damp and cold with old perspiration. He lies still.*]

GARY: . . . I don't fancy much Firestone's chances of getting home to Buckingham Palace tonight!

[*RAINE and BEV.*

RAINE touches BEV's arm.]

RAINE: Makes you go clammy in here.

BEV: In the street on a normal day when yer in uniform people stand off. Down in the tube though, it's different.

RAINE: I like the London Underground.

BEV: I don't. When I'm in uniform, I wait for the end compartment of the train where there's least people. I find that in the rush hour they like to catch you in a crush. It's your uniform. And they lean right up against you. Right up hard. As if they just want to, you know . . .

RAINE: It's all right, Bev.

BEV: Eh?

RAINE: It's all right. Nobody's going to touch you now.

BEV: Pardon?

[*RAINE is alert to some inner doubt of BEV's. RAINE is quick there.*

DARRYL gestures to BEV to help him with his clobber. RAINE helps GARY with his pads. GARY and DARRYL look odd in their bodices.]

GARY: . . . I suppose Driss has gone back to find another key.

RAINE: Where would he go?

GARY: He must have a place where they got spare keys like.

DARRYL: He'll fetch an expert with him. He'll wait until all *them* has gone. And it's quiet then. He's a canny one.

BEV: Course he'll be back, Gary, course he'll be.

RAINE: We know that, Bev. Hardly is he going to leave us all night.

KEVIN: I wouldn't mind if he did.

GARY: Kev. Belt up!

[*The GIRLS go behind the curtain, to undress. The BOYS are in states of undress, bodice tops, y-fronts and leggings, certain ugly picture.*]

DARRYL [*to* KEVIN]: When . . . you get to Belfast, mate, they'll put you in a room no bigger than a cupboard, with eight bunks. No window. An electrically operated fan through a grill. They give you an Armalite with a Weaver-type night scan attachment. It helps you see in the dark for five hundred yards. You don't have to worry about that. And you don't have to worry about sharing your cupboard with the nignog lads. The staff officer puts the black soldiers in one cupboard. And if we're lucky it's these black boys who get sent down the Falls at night. It's easier for them. They can't be seen in the dark anyway. And it's better for us because we can get a normal night's kip. Mind you, some shits get a bit nervy about this sort of thing back home. There was a black soldier trod on something nasty outside the Mickey Sloane Working Men's Club. Lay there until morning. Then we had to send in the wheelbarrow to test the body for boobies. And this American Yank this photographer tried to take some snaps of the body. The NCO confiscated his camera on the spot. Later the British Army Press Desk put out to the effect that the film was blank on account the bloke hadn't bothered to take his lens cap off. I don't want to see a photo of a black head dying in Belfast. Do you? I mean – what's the world coming to? Eh? It ain' that they're black I mind, it's that they get very black when they get black about fings . . . or somefin . . . what? . . .

[*Tiredness and relaxed, all.*]

RAINE: . . . Sorry, Bev.

BEV: What for?

RAINE: It's easier for you girls to let off steam. In camp I'm watched all the time. Is she getting wed? Is she a les? Has she been passed up? Who's taking her place? My lot that is.

GARY [*mimicking* DRISS]: . . . This is Charley Tango Bravo, this is Charley Tango Bravo. We are all trapped in this Personnel Carrier, P for Personnel and C for Carrier, practising the art of Mas. Where was I?

[KEVIN *stands. Looks mysterious. Something deep within him.*]

KEVIN: . . . Listen.

GARY: Hallo, it's Kev.

KEVIN: Ssh!

DARRYL: Wot?

KEVIN: Can't you hear. . .?

GARY: No.

[*ALICE steps forward. A bra on. Little else. A shirt around her waist. All the clothes askew.*]

ALICE: They've almost gone.

[*They listen. Distant carnival echoes; the drums and the floats and the forces of victory away off now.*]

KEVIN: Long way off now?

[*RAINE comes out. Bra and pants and shaven head. She opens two of the little slit windows. Breathes in deep.*]

RAINE: . . . Heaven ay? Lovely fresh air, come in!

[*Their spirits commence to rise. A greater relaxation. GARY goes behind the aisle curtain. And returns wearing RAINE's wig. Just as RAINE smiles at her girls –*]

I could shower you all with kisses!

GARY [*in wig*]: . . . Could you?

[*She looks round at him. Goes up to him. Plants big wet one. Then RAINE steps away a little uneasily. As if she has never really done that too often in the past. GARY wants more, natch. But it is not on offer. She ducks his arms and reaches for GARY's khaki jacket. She slings it on loosely. There she is in her underwear with her bald pate still on her head and this half-slung army fatigue jacket.*]

RAINE [*to GARY*]: I feel a bit safer in a khaki jacket . . . you don't mind, Gary?

GARY [*forward*]: . . . Raine. . .

RAINE: Yes, Gary?

GARY: Don't I get a bit more than – ?

RAINE [*fends him away gently*]: 'Fraid not. . . see – not really too keen on boys, see.

GARY: Well, nor am I.

RAINE [*gentle, but firm*]: . . . I fuck girls, Gary.

GARY [*in his tracks, stopped*]: . . . Excuse me?

[*GARY is very alone. But RAINE is nice. She wipes lipstick from his mouth. Looks a little agape though.*]

DARRYL [*to* GARY]: So who's a pretty boy then ain' goin' to get his tonight! Excuse me!

GARY: I'll 'ave yoo, Lance Corporal!

KEVIN: Sssh!

[*He leans against the wall of the bus to listen. They all listen with him.*

One final dink in the atoms of the ear comes through to us from the carnival. Somewhere way up there on the hill away from us a dink like a last couple of bars from the heroes-of-victory floats a lifting lilt of jah root satisfaction derisive and cocky at one and the same moment. And the music ceases.

They wait a beat.]

GARY: I fink . . .

[*He is at a loss. Those last words of* RAINE'S. *He hovers.*]

I'll go and check that canister where you stoopid put it.

[ALICE *shrugs as he passes her.* GARY *goes to the back of the bus to check the suitcase.*

He comes back evidently satisfied.

ALICE *puts her arm around* KEVIN.]

BEV: . . . Quiet now, init . . . ?

RAINE: Heaven . . .

DARRYL [*reaching for his sack*]: That official, Sarge, is it?

RAINE: Why not!

DARRYL: Special Duty Patrol dismiss, Sarge?

RAINE: Right! Corporal!

[DARRYL *pulls out a number of loose cans of beer. Each beer has a ring top lid. They are assorted types of beer. Noticeably all of a smaller kind – no tall lager cans which are too bulky.*

DARRYL *fetches out a small cassette and chucks a couple of cartridges on the bench seat behind him. He squats on the floor surrounded by his cans of beer.*]

DARRYL: Step to it, Private bloody Simpkin!

[GARY *takes from his sack another pile of small beer cans.*

DARRYL *presses the cassette machine. Rod Stewart emerges. But for the time being it is very faint.*

RAINE *and* BEV *stand the cans up in a line. And* DARRYL

commences to unzip the tops and place them in another line. He does several.

BEV *still has her rollers on her feet. The coloured hair and the bright face paint. Although in a state of weird undress she has somehow managed to keep her Nazi dagger belt with its symbols.*

DARRYL *is busy opening the cans. He hardly looks down at them. He does it by finger touch.* BEV *piles up more cans for him. It is clear the boys intend to drink twenty or so each.*]

DARRYL: Well . . . Bev . . . after twenty of these, I'm all yours. My lovely body will be entirely at your disposal to do with what you fancy.

BEV: I don't know how to put this to you, Darryl, it doesn't normally require half a gallon of beer to clock up the steam to offer me anything!

DARRYL: I'm sayin' I'm sayin' –

BEV: I'm not that unattractive such that it requires twenty Newcastle Browns before you can crank up your camshaft.

DARRYL: You're looking at the quickest pint downer and fastest can opener in the 17th Infantry canteen!

[BEV *slams more cans down for him to open.*]

BEV: . . . Sorry, Darryl. I am not having a one-night stand with four hundred cans of beer. And if you can open them all up blindfold, and your big left toe up your rear end – I don't give a widow twankey's!

DARRYL: You're mad about me, aren't you?

[KEVIN *follows* ALICE *inside the back portion beyond the curtain. He takes her another beer.* BEV'*s face paint is dripping.*

DARYL *and helmeted* GARY *and* BEV *and* RAINE *take up temporary positions.* DARRYL *raises a Rod Stewart track. Not loud. They drink.*

ALICE *and* KEVIN *sit at a double seat. It is placed in such a way they could not notice anything strange happening to the bench seat the canister is placed in.*]

KEVIN: Two year ago my older brother Jessie did his first four months overseas in this Turkish place NATO Corridor Pact. Then they sent him to Munich. When he come back to home his wife only has a kid knocked up by somebody else. He spends five months lookin' for a job, and there was none. One day, on his tod he went and re-applied for a three-year posting in the army. They turned him down. Somfin' about the state of his mind bein' disturbed. So he said sod that, an' tied a washing machine hosepipe on to his exhaust, an' he sat in the back of his van with the engine runnin'. He sat there holdin' on to this piece of hose. He sat there for six bloody hours, waiting to go, when he discovered he'd left a cold air fan switched on all this time. So that oxygen kept comin' in all the time. Shortly after that, he become extremely potty, and they come an' took him away ... I'm a virgin, Alice.

ALICE: I think ... I'm coming out in a heat rash all over my chest.

KEVIN: Rash?

ALICE: Rash.

[*She nods.* KEVIN *smiles with her. He pulls a blanket up over the pair of them. Heads and bodies on the seat. His head is towards the audience more on top of her. The blanket covers them completely.*

DARRYL'*s cassette finishes one song. A beat, then – the opening bars of ' Sailing ' commence.*

DARRYL *raises the sound. Each one of the four in the front –* RAINE *and* BEV, *and* DARRYL *and* GARY *take up different positions.*

As if they are all going to sing along with the music. Each one adopts a pose. Comfortable but strange.

The underwear, the wigs, the boots, naked legs and arms, leggings, bodices, bras and pants, bright hair and bizarre face paint, BEV *in her roller skates and* RAINE *with her CS cartridge belt and khaki jacket. Obscene tableau.*

Behind the aisle curtain KEVIN *is making movements with his body. It appears he is on top but not wholly in charge of the operation.*

After a few opening bars and the definition of the melody, all four in the front singalong with Rod. They are not a very tuneful choir. The song if anything provides DARRYL *with a release of energy. The* GIRLS *are out of key.*

68

GARY *still has the wig on. He picks up* RAINE'*s lipstick.*
Colours lips. RAINE *nods.* GARY *and* RAINE *hold hands and*
dance closely.
BEV *and* DARRYL *commence a tit-and-bum grind.*
DARRYL *trips and collapses.*
BEV'*s head on* RAINE'*s shoulder.* RAINE'*s protective arm.*]

RAINE/BEV/DARRYL/GARY:

'I am sailing
I am sailing
        home again across the sea.
I am sailing
        stormy waters
to be with you to be free . . .'

[*The case where* ALICE *hid the gashed CS canister com-*
mences to expand. It is an unusual action because it is slow
and it does not immediately catch the eye.]

RAINE/BEV/DARRYL/GARY:

'I am flying
I am flying
        like a bird across the sky.
I am flying
        passing high clouds
to be near you to be free . . .'

[*The suitcase snaps open behind them. The CS canister*
inside the plastic bag wrap commences to expand. Fast. It is
black and bulbous and a growth.]

RAINE/BEV/DARRYL/GARY:

'Can you hear me?
can you hear me?
        through the dark clouds far away.
I am dying forever crying
to be with you – who can say?

Can you hear me?
Can you hear me? . . .'

[*The CS gas grows out of all proportion and it has taken on*
the appearance of a balloon. It continues to expand.
Neither those in the front of the bus can see the seat ex-
pansion because of the aisle curtain.

Nor can ALICE *or* KEVIN *under their blanket see it even if they pulled the blanket aside. Prone as they are and occupied as they are.*]

RAINE/BEV/DARRYL/GARY:

'We are sailing

We are sailing

             home again across the sea . . . '

[*The blanket breaks loose of* KEVIN'*s face. He looks outwards. He wears an expression of seraphic confidence. He joins in –*]

KEVIN: 'I am sailing

I am sailing . . . '

RAINE/BEV/DARRYL/GARY:

'We are sailing

We are sailing

             home again across the sea

We are sailing

             stormy waters

to be near you to be free.

Oh my Lord

             to be near you to be free.

Oh my Lord

             to be near you to be free.

Oh my Lord

             to be near you to be free.

Oh my Lord . . . '

[*The CS plastic black balloon reaches an alarming circumference.*

They stop singing on the last chorus.

Different lights inside the bus.

Their still positions. Ugly and Frozen.

Lights on their faces. Streaked and gaudy paint.

Lights on the balloon of gas.

Lights on their bodies strewn across the bus, tiredness and perspiration.

The final chords of the music.]

FADE.

Midnite at the Starlite

'In the late bourgeois world of today, when the class problem has become so intense, art tends to be divorced from social ideas, to drive the individual still further into his desperate alienation, to encourage an impotent egoism, and to turn reality into a false myth, surrounded by the magic rites of a bogus cult.'

ERNST FISCHER, 1959

Midnite at the Starlite was first performed at the Birmingham Repertory Studio Theatre on 5 February 1981 with the following cast:

Gerry Hawking	PETER SALLIS
The Organizer	MARIA CHARLES
Avril Vickers	SHEILA KELLEY
Artie Vickers	CHRISTOPHER ETTRIDGE
Dot Dooly	YVONNE EDGELL
Trevis Comport	BARRY PHILIPS

Directed by Pill Pryde
Designed by Geoffrey Scott
Costumes by Ann Curtis
Choreographed by Peter Maxwell

CHARACTERS

AVRIL VICKERS, thirties.

ARTIE VICKERS, thin and wiry. Has a distinctive baldness.

DOT DOOLY, twenties.

TREVIS COMPORT, twenties. Bruising manner. Beneath toupé has identical hair-line to Artie.

THE ORGANIZER, ladylike.

GERRY HAWKING, late fifties.

THE BAND is not imagined as a full ten-man group. The music is heard at a distaff measure. For example, *equale brass* can be made up of two trombones, a cello and a side drum. The effect, with popular dance numbers, is intended to be ironic and witty, and yet formal.

ACT ONE

A dressing-room. A section of ballroom floor. A decorative entranceway with draped curtains and swish. A number of gilt chairs and tables. A mirrorball. Dressing-room tannoy.

[*Car door clicks.*
Back door to the dressing-room snaps.
ARTIE *carries a sewing-machine into the dressing-room.*
AVRIL *catches up with him. She drags two heavy cases.*]

AVRIL: . . . Artie!

ARTIE: My love?

AVRIL: The car door!

ARTIE: Ah.

AVRIL: The corridor door!

ARTIE: Mm.

AVRIL: The car keys?

ARTIE: Eh.

AVRIL: The sewing-machine is much lighter than these bloody two!

[*She drops the cases.*]

ARTIE: Sewing-machines need to be placed down gently.

AVRIL: Why are you rushing about like . . . ?

ARTIE: I am at my normal pace.

AVRIL: We're not in a race!

[*She boots the nearest suitcase.*]

ARTIE: Go easy with that one – me three pairs of patents are in that one and they're not with their trees on – the way you kick it.

AVRIL [*pause*]: . . . And I'm worried about the babysitter. It is not responsible to leave a couple of kids with a fifteen-year-old babysitter who's as thick as Dutch clogs.

ARTIE: She's a very big fifteen-year-old.

AVRIL: Big? So?

ARTIE: She's big enough to fool the next-door neighbour. I've seen his eyes go funny when he clocks that T-shirt.

AVRIL: It's illegal to have her in the house alone.

ARTIE: It's illegal to have her anywhere alone –

AVRIL: Very cheap that one. She is illegal.

ARTIE: We can't afford the agency. She's half the price. We have to find a way to get by.

AVRIL: If the house burns down you can go to gaol.

[*She swans out. He doesn't notice.*]

ARTIE [*alone*]: . . . The garage will not burn down . . . the children will not be incinerated in the attic . . . with a bit of luck my patent shoes will not crack because I keep them at foot temperature on the second shelf of the airing cupboard . . . and I will not go to gaol because on the whole I spend most of me time and energy keeping me wife in the dance competitions she has become accustomed to . . . Avril?

[*AVRIL carries a Spanish dress in a fold-back transparent sheath, and two balloons of taffeta dresses – one pink, one blue. She stands in the doorway from the corridor. The dress over her shoulder is close to the jamb.*]

AVRIL [*as if she has not stopped*]: And . . . Lord live with you night and day – I want a proper explanation of why you will never invite mother back into the house to look after the kids when she has so often promised to? Begged to? What? I've despaired – yes, despaired – so often at your past attitude to mum. She knows what we do every night. And she is dying to look after the kids for us. If you don't talk to me about mum I'm going to – I don't know what I – I'll kick you so hard you won't chassé all night. Honest –

[*As she advances, the inside taffeta unrolls like a bog roll. It is caught somewhere out in the passage. She realizes too late.*]

[*softly*]: . . . Artie? . . .

ARTIE: Yes, dearest?

AVRIL: Je suis disarrey.

ARTIE: Yais?

AVRIL: Disastre.

ARTIE [*looking up*]: . . . My Christ . . . don't move . . .

AVRIL: I'm in the pink one tonight.

ARTIE: Not tonight. Pink's gone for el burton, matey mate.

AVRIL: Blue is unlucky for me, on Mondays. I never wear blue first day of the week.

ARTIE: Nice, init? You only need Artie when there's the old crisis.

AVRIL: That was the intention of our marriage vows, wasn't it?

ARTIE: Was it? When?

AVRIL: Am I going to call for help? I got six dances lined up for the pink and we ought not to be discussing children, marriages and my mum at this moment in time.

ARTIE: Stand still . . .

[*He goes outside. The taffeta stays taut.*]

[*offstage*]: My Lor an' ows yer farver!

AVRIL: We shouldn't be talking like this just before . . .

ARTIE [*offstage*]: Don't advance or retire.

AVRIL: All this talk about mother . . .

ARTIE [*offstage*]: Don't promenade a hair on your head.

AVRIL: What you've never let into your skull is the fact that mum would make living cheaper if she . . .

[ARTIE *steps back in with a bundle of pink taff.*]

ARTIE: Your mum does not love me.

AVRIL: But she does the kids.

ARTIE: I am not married to her. And I see no prospect of that unlikely union ever occurring.

[*They pause. She stares him out.*

ARTIE *sets up the sewing-machine. He plugs the cord in. Sits before it.*]

AVRIL: I want it done in time. I am pink tonight.

ARTIE: I do me all.

AVRIL: I . . . apologize. For talking out of turn. About things.

ARTIE: And anyway why are there those two cases? I packed my gear in yours.

AVRIL: I just think . . . we never got started right, right at the start . . .

ARTIE: In future never ask Dot to machine your snags. She never finishes off on ends. And she lets the bodkin run out and never reloads. Don't rely on Dot for anything.

AVRIL [*tenser*]: The bloke is coming to mend the washing-machine at twelve tomorrow morning.

ARTIE [*engrossed in the machine*]: Ah.

AVRIL: There is a very good reason, based on decades of domestic science research, why that hoover won't work on the top stair turn.

ARTIE [*needle and arm in place now*]: Mm.

AVRIL: The last time mum came to stay you spent the entire weekend in a tent on the garage floor. Since that day I've never seen the key to the garage, ever.

ARTIE: You were where, dear?

AVRIL: Artie, before the others come –

[ARTIE *switches on the sewing-machine and rattles through the taffeta. He pulls the strips of pink at a lick. He doubles over the end thread. And switches off. He turns.*]

ARTIE: . . . You were saying?

[*Lights change on the dressing-room.*

TREVIS, *in black motorcycle tack, plus helmet and bag, slumps on a delicate gilt chair.*

GERRY *fetches a standing microphone and places it in the MC's corner, where there is a hint of a band podium.* GERRY *plugs the mike in. Sees the outline of* TREVIS. *Hesitates. Walks across the ballroom floor. Empty squeaks of cracked patents.*

TREVIS's *bag balances the plastic suit sheath with its all-weather cover.*]

GERRY: Jitters, jitters, have we?

TREVIS: Eh?

GERRY: For tonight?

TREVIS: No, we haven't.

GERRY: Pale ale in the cheeks, then?

TREVIS: If you don't mind – cobblers.

GERRY: Do I know that one? Old-time three step, was it?

TREVIS: 'Scuse me.

GERRY: Have we met before?

TREVIS: That awful notion has already crossed me mind.

GERRY: That Deptford Formation Christmas Eve Dance Competition in aid of the Vietnam boat people? When that big girl's left wobbly fell out of her cross-your-knees thing?

TREVIS: Yearh, I was there.

GERRY: Don't you remember the MC?

TREVIS: No. Sorry.

GERRY: Me, me!

TREVIS: As the MC wore a ton of white feathers, a sort of grosgrain tutu pair of Y-fronts and a Mother Goose nose hardly is it I would have.

GERRY: What a memory. Me, me, that was!

TREVIS: The only time in me life I've seen the MC trying to get on his points in a pair of black wellies filled with lager right up to the knees.

GERRY: We are very muscular today.

TREVIS: Had a bad day.

GERRY: Commiserate I say, shake out the tears, let the little things in life hang out, someone somewhere is sure to take a fancy.

TREVIS: A terrible weekend . . . an' all . . .

GERRY: Daren't ask any more.

TREVIS: A filthy week before that.

GERRY: Really?

TREVIS: And before that – a whole month of it.

GERRY: I know – you're married, but it isn't working out.

TREVIS [pause]: . . . Yes. No. What's it to you?

GERRY: You look the type.

TREVIS: What does that mean?

GERRY: Dark and muscular and rather . . . dare I say?

TREVIS: Go on, dare?

GERRY: A bit over the top with it. Too outfront.

[TREVIS adjusts his black riding two-piece. The zips glint.]

. . . If you see.

TREVIS: No . . .

GERRY: You ever been a swimwear model?

TREVIS: No.

GERRY: That's how I see you.

TREVIS: Don't give me tha—

79

GERRY: Really.

TREVIS: Narh...

GERRY: All the way up those escalators in the Piccadilly Underground, in those little frame box photos.

TREVIS: Why Piccadilly?

GERRY: You'll be asking for my address next.

TREVIS: No, mate.

GERRY: Well, that's a pity. I was on the verge of putting it out on offer.

TREVIS: I do not want to be propositioned.

GERRY: Everybody wants to be propositioned. You don't deny yourself, do you? Are you one of those modern martyr types? The arrows in the closet type. Saintly?

TREVIS: I don't deny meself anything. But there is a limit to what I can take.

GERRY: We are fully booked up for the early evenings.

TREVIS: Blood is rushing to the back of me head, I've got a tingling sensation in me boots, and me fist is curling up.

GERRY: Oh, bold.

TREVIS: I mean it, darling!

GERRY: Course you do – you're prickly. They all are.

TREVIS: Who... said I'm gay?

GERRY: Who said you're not?

TREVIS: What makes you think you can trot to conclusions like that? Haven't you seen motorcycle gear before? Just because I've a couple dozen zips on me it doesn't mean I'm on offer all round.

GERRY: I can see something in your eye, sailor, ever so small, but there it is.

TREVIS: Thank you, I'll stick to me eyedrops. It's nice the way you got yer knickers in a twist, init? Eh? Just because I'm here to dance it don't mean I'm a left-handed five-shilling pound note.

GERRY [*looking*]: ... Mm.

TREVIS: Anyway... leave off... enough problems...

GERRY: ... Mmm.

[TREVIS *climbs out of his black top. Bold T-shirt beneath. Hairy chest.*]

GERRY: What's your speciality, then? Are you competing or doing a demonstration?

TREVIS: I *was* entered for the comp.

GERRY: What's up?

TREVIS: She's just late, that's all. She may never turn up, and I've paid for the entries.

GERRY: Wife's not here? Small mercies I say.

TREVIS: I don't dance with her like. I dance with someone else.

GERRY: Really?

TREVIS: She dances with another partner. I just dance with somebody else's wife.

GERRY: One of those, is it? Emotions everywhere, and you don't know your quick from your slow. Life is less exhausting and uncomplicated if you keep your handbag over your heart and shop about a bit for the joy.

TREVIS: Eh?

GERRY: If you don't mind me saying so – I don't think you're a hetero at all.

TREVIS: Me fist is tightening.

GERRY: It's just the idea you like.

TREVIS: How bloody dare you.

GERRY: Don't take it amiss – the adjudicators are not here to judge you for that, dear.

[TREVIS *grabs* GERRY *by the throat.*]

TREVIS: Now look!

[TREVIS *waves his fist.*]

GERRY: Outrage, dear, is the best come-on in the business.

[*Lights down.*

Lights again on the dressing-room door. THE ORGANIZER *in her long gown trips along with score sheets, indexes of partners, etc. She pins a dance sheet against the dressing-room door. She puts up a similar card beside the ornate curtain entrance.*

Lights on TREVIS, *alone.*

DOT *carries a zip bag for her Latin dress, and a draped ballroom dress over her arm; she has an extra bag and a suitcase with her. She steps up behind* TREVIS. *She kisses him. He does not look round.*]

DOT: Trev, darling ... ?

TREVIS: Where were you last night?

DOT: I went for a walk, darling.

TREVIS: All bloody night walk, did you?

DOT: It was a long walk, yes, darling.

TREVIS: How far can you go in the pouring rain from midnight till half past seven in the morning? This morning? I got up to shave and get off for work, and you'd just bloody come in. I could tell. I saw you on the settee. Your heels gave you away – they were still hot. How far can you walk in the rain in satin stilettoes? How far can you go in a little black dress made of nothing?

DOT: Now don't get ratty, Trevis, you know how it upsets your tempo.

TREVIS: Who did you sleep with last night?

DOT: We have a pact, remember?

TREVIS: Where was it this time? An MG Midget, was it? With the stilettoes up through the canvas roof? What was on the old cassette then? The New Hawaiians' Go Latin, was it? I can just see this MG Midget in the pissing rain, parked discreetly on Upper Tooting, yer legs through the roof, and this vehicle throbbing with a sort of grass-skirted Honolulu samba. Oh yes.

DOT: I live in your little flat, Trev. But I am not yet wed. Just the same as we don't dance as partners on the floor in comps, you prefer to dance with Avril.

TREVIS: Avril happens to be my perfect dancing partner on the floor.

DOT: Anyway, I've come back.

TREVIS: If you hadn't have turned up, I'd have vomited from the internal acid in my stomach. I wouldn't have been able to dance with Av, and she would have lost this chance for the Streatham Park-Tooting Bec Common final. Don't you understand the importance of tonight? It's the ace partners night for the entire London Ballroom Section of SW 17. SW 17 is no allotment patch for club-footed Morris dancers. This is the steaming crème buille of the old cream. And you seem to deliberately want to sabotage my morale.

DOT: There's mine, too.

TREVIS: My morale, I'm talking about my morale – at a low ebb. And if my physical and mental well-being is on a down, my artistic tempo hits the floor with it. I'm ambitious with Avril because we know we can succeed. Where did we reach at the Winter Towers, Clacton Pier, last Michaelmas? Bloody fifteenth out of all East Essex Young Marrieds. And I wasn't even married. And who was on the adjudicating panel? Dmitri Bender no less, and Gwenethe Lavelle! Dmitri's Vice Chairman of the International Federation of Ballrooms. And Gwenethe's a Fellow of the British Association of Tap Dancers.

DOT: Well, darling, here I am, darling, I love you loads of pash and kisses, darling, and you and Av are sure to get to the South London trials. It may be only SW 17 tonight, but it's the world tomorrow, Trev, right?

TREVIS: I didn't sleep a wink last night with worry. My lower pectorals have stiffened up so much, they feel like plastic patent left out in the sun. And as for my artistic tempo –

DOT: I've trampled it to death, darling.

TREVIS: Trampled.

DOT: Don't worry, Trev. You'll win. You'll be popular. You'll get the Under Thirties Youth Award. They'll love you.

TREVIS: Don't destroy me, Dot. I'm all I've got left.

[GERRY *emerges from the side of the floor. He approaches them.*]

... You're carrying an awful load of gear?

DOT: No ... don't think so.

GERRY [*to* DOT]: ... Hallo, dear. I'm Gerry Hawking. Your MC tonight. M for mother, C for charley. Never mind. Perhaps me deaf grandmother one will raise a tit. [*to* TREVIS] Now I recall where it was.

TREVIS: What was?

GERRY: Where you and me met.

TREVIS: I don't remember and we never did.

GERRY [*to* DOT]: Shy one, this – is he yours for the time being?

TREVIS: Me fist's curling.

GERRY: I hadn't got used to seeing you with clothes on. It

was Brockwell Park Baths last summer. That was it, you devil. Confess.

TREVIS: What to?

GERRY: You were fetching in those stretch stars and stripes trunks.

TREVIS: I work at Brockwell Park Baths as the swimming attendant and junior coach. I do possess a pair of Ronald Reagan trunks.

GERRY: Yes, well, you looked wonderful. All the year round, is it?

TREVIS: I start work in the spring.

GERRY: Like the lambs do.

TREVIS: It's seasonal.

GERRY [*to* DOT]: When I saw him he was taking bets on how many hand-stand steps he could do along a row of upright deckchairs.

DOT: Oh he loves to display himself.

GERRY: I just knew.

TREVIS [*to* DOT]: Shadap.

> [*Lights down.*
> *Lights cast in two places.* GERRY *is at the edge of the podium where the band might sit with the microphone.*
> *Opposite him, alone, stands* THE ORGANIZER *in her evening dress. She watches* GERRY.]

GERRY [*clears throat*]: . . . Lights please!

> [*Lights fetch out more of the ballroom floor, the 'Midnite at the Starlite' motifs in lovely garishness, the silvery panoply of the occasion.*]

. . . Good evening, Modern Ballroom Dance lovers. Testing, testing. The Streatham Park and Tooting Bec night for selection to higher things outside our little SW 17. We can't all stay seventeen for ever, nor south-west etcetera. Is there an ill-winds' joke somewhere in that? We have tonight a special panel of adjudicators who will score for us. There will be six strict tempo events. The adjudication will be out of five for each dance. We have fourteen couples from all kinds of affiliated bodies. Testing, testing. Bodies, bodies.

A round welcome of applause to us all for our Midnite at the renowned Starlite. Our scrutineer for the evening will be Donny Atherton, IDTA and FISTD. You'll all remember Donny as the triple champion in the South Australian All Asian Latin Champs 1956. There will be a sequence demonstration by two couples from the Top Rank Suite, Swansea. Two cups will be awarded on an accumulative count system approved by the Ballroom Dancers Federation. There will also be our traditional booby prize. One regulation army boot with half a bottle of champagne-type bubbly for the funniest step of the evening.

... Blues please!

[*Lights turn to blue. The new hue makes a feature of the corner.*]

[*he reads from cards*] ... We have a couple from the Catford Bus Depot. Peggy and Eric Greave. Both members of the Transport and General Workers Union. Both bus drivers, Peggy and Eric, so they should give us no trouble with their 'passing reverses'. The couple we ought to give a glad hand to, Mervyn and Estelle, are in fact newcomers to our shore. This couple hail all the way from St Kitts in the Caribbean, and they have studied ballroom technique by means of postal tuition and Victor Silvester's portable floor plans. Mervyn's first lessons were conducted on the golden beaches of the Caribbean with the aid of a cassette player. They live on Leigham Court Avenue, and Mervyn is a GLC parking meter attendant. Their preferences are for the waltz tempo, and Estelle grows, in the privacy of her windowbox, a variety of Olde English roses. Their favourite dance number is 'Footsteps in the Sand'.

... Pinks please!

[*Lights obey.*]

... I'll record one delightful message, our great friends Janice and Carl Merridean gave birth to an eight-pound baby boy this morning, to be named Roy Carl Charles. According to doting mum he's already perfected his 'basic movements' and will come out of the maternity ward dancing all the way. Janice and Carl intend to resume their heavy duties with the Tooting Bec Formation Reelers the moment young Roy gives them a night off.

... Go for gold!

[*Lights obey.*]

... There will be a whip-round for all aficionados for the European Fund in aid of persuading the International Olympic Committee to recognize Modern Ballroom Dancing as a legitimate Olympic event. After all, the ancient Greeks were out there dancing on Olympus before the marathon had begun. Give generously, boys and girls. We must be prepared to put our pockets where our feet are ... oh dear ... ... Mirrorball please!

[*Mirrorball sways into position. It gives a hurtling starry garishness to the hues.*]

... So I must bring to a close our wonderful Midnite at the Starlite for all our SW 17 Modern Ballroom Dance lovers. Maestro Bob Willer-Paisley and his Paul Whiteman Naturals will lead us on out with 'The Last Waltz'. Everybody will thank, I'm sure, our judges and our competitors, in a big round hand. And I want us all out on the floor, don't I? In 'The Last Waltz'. And that means you, darling, you there trying to pretend your patents don't squeak – everyone on to the floor! Goodnight! Goodnight! Goodnight!

[*He waves at the vacant floor.*

Inside the dressing-room. AVRIL *and* DOT. TREVIS *and* ARTIE. *They are changing and preparing.*

THE ORGANIZER *bustles in. She holds the back number cards for the contestants.*]

ORGANIZER: Now, dears, I don't need to tell you that you now are in the married couples' locker room. This is not me usual experience of comps. I mean under any normal circumstances the boys keep to the boys' room and the girls to the girls'. Right and proper. But this locker-room lot here is absolutely hopeless. There just isn't enough space. That is why we've made a concession to modernity and placed husbands and wives together. I can only apologize that you are still forced to share a locker like this.

DOT: That's all right. We four have known each other for years. We're always together anyway.

ORGANIZER: So without any further ado – let's make life simple – we are all married, aren't we?

DOT: Er ...

ORGANIZER: I do hope so. There are so many public spats in modern life. The reason why the singles' lockers get so crowded is they're all fully booked with divorcees and the like, and there's no end to it.

TREVIS: We are all married, thank you!

ORGANIZER: Avril and Artie Vickers, please?

AVRIL/ARTIE: Yes. That's us.

ORGANIZER: Dorothy Dooly and Trevis Comport?

DOT: Yes.

TREVIS: I'm Trevis.

ORGANIZER: You are Dorothy's husband?

TREVIS: Yes.

ORGANIZER: And Dorothy is legally married?

TREVIS: Yes.

ORGANIZER: Dorothy is in real life Mrs Comport?

TREVIS: Yes.

ORGANIZER: Dorothy likes to use her maiden name, is that it?

TREVIS: Yes.

ORGANIZER: Oh, what a relief.

[THE ORGANIZER *gives the number '9' white square to* DOT.]

ORGANIZER: Mr and Mrs Comport, number '9'.

DOT: I don't dance with my husband.

ORGANIZER: Then who do you dance with, dear?

ARTIE: She dances with me.

ORGANIZER: Number '6' is then for ... ?

AVRIL: Mr Comport and me.

ORGANIZER: In the old days, married couples made the best dancers. Partners on the floor, partners off.

ARTIE: Oh that was donkeys' tails ago. What happened when the Grizzly Bear and the Funky Butt came in? All change. Things got a bit neither here nor there when the great Arthur Murray had his divorce. What a scandal that was.

The dancing fraternity and the *Ballroom Times* held its breath. World ballroom morale wobbled.

ORGANIZER: We never discussed Arthur Murray's divorce.

ARTIE: And what about Victor Silvester, eh?

ORGANIZER: What about Victor Silvester?

ARTIE: Oh yes, what about Victor Silvester, you know!

ORGANIZER: In my day, we always looked to better things for the art. There was a time, years before you lot, when the actual Prince of Wales was seriously interested in the Black Bottom. It was such an aficionado talking point and I remember when Guy Lombardo actually got the Prince himself on to the floor at the Trocadero Tea Party Dance. There was Jack Buchanan, Gilda Gray, Annette Mills and Bobbie Sielle no less. The entire weight of the dancing leaders of the day were leaning on the Prince with all their influence, that day.

ARTIE: As he was flat-footed, stone-deaf, pigeon-toed and three foot tall, it's a wonder they didn't have him laid out like a pancake.

ORGANIZER: Leaning on the Prince with a view towards influencing his decision as to how to give the dancing world maximum prestige. If Jack Buchanan had married Unity Mitford and had strong words with Adolf Hitler, World War Two never would have happened. Jack would have been knighted. Unity would have become a national hero. And the Prince of Wales would have become patron to the dancing fraternity. Instead, what have we got? A bunch of dowdy royals, who occupy most of their day patting corgis and caressing steeplechasers. Jack dashed his chances when the hopes of the dancing world lay on his shoulders. He dabbled with a Latin lady in Acapulco and there was an unfortunate item of publicity about his income tax. Blithe hopes.

ARTIE: I mean nowadays couples dance as partners, and yet they've been divorced for years. They've remarried again. But they still keep to the same instructor and the same comps. There they are – full of hate and revulsion for one another in private life – out there on the floor smashing through the Formation Awards. Some couples never as much as speak when off the floor. Other couples, who have nice normal separate families, actually conduct passionate affairs out on the floor. Out there, under the spot, partaking in an orgy you couldn't equal at the Southport Hydro on a Saturday night. It's a bit different now.

ORGANIZER: Is it?

ARTIE: I knew a couple once who were so allergic to each other – you know there just wasn't a single thing in the physical repertoire which went well. One skin was clammy, the other was dry. One liked garlic, the other liked cloves. One perspired under the arms, the other did it in his patents. There wasn't an item of communication they shared in common off the floor. But when the lights came down, and they got into the Gainsborough Glide, brother it was all over. They could step out – veleta-like – with diagonals and pivots you wouldn't find on a humming-top. Magic. With hate and loathing all the way. Suffering and splendour and blood out there on the Canadian maple-leaf floor. Tremendous.

ORGANIZER: You'll be called twice, for each dance. I'll knock and shout, and then I'll just shout. Enter and exit under the arcade curtains. No standing around waiting for the adjudicator's eye. Results will be relayed via the tannoy. All contestants will be required out on the floor, once the dances have finished, to hear the cumulative decision of the judges. You'll be expected to stay in your costumes for the last waltz. You do not dance to the National Anthem. All clothes and possessions must be removed from here by one a.m., when the cleaner arrives. No drinking in the room. No rowdy behaviour. And no running from one changing-room to the other. Anything reported stolen must be subject to intensive inquiries later. Any questions?

AVRIL: Can we ask the names of the judges alongside the adjudicator?

ORGANIZER: No you can't.

ARTIE [*to* THE ORGANIZER]: What you do all this for, love? Bring it all back like for you?

ORGANIZER: Mr Hawking and myself often officiate dos.

TREVIS: Hawking? The MC?

ORGANIZER: Mr Hawking is my husband.

TREVIS: Eh?

ORGANIZER: Although we are married, we don't like to trumpet it about, especially during competitions.

TREVIS: 'Scuse I – will there be a press photographer?

ORGANIZER: *South London Press* has been invited. They never come to this grade. *Dancing Times* said they were mildly interested in the demonstration dancers from Swansea. Transport and General Workers' house magazine photographer said he'd come. Salmond Brothers Hired Outfitters, Streatham High, were coming, but their camera was stolen at the Cricklewood Ten Pin Palais last week. It happened during the Amateur Latins.

[*She shuts the door behind her.*]

DOT: Who did you expect, Trev? TV cameras, was it?

ARTIE: That'll be the day.

TREVIS: Maybe it will.

DOT: Here, Trev darling – I liked the bit about being married, darling.

TREVIS: I saw from the look on that old trout's face – one word wrong, and they'd split us up. My nerves are already suffering from enough artiste's tempo. I'm at a pitch.

DOT: Go on!

ARTIE: After all, Dot, we don't often share a room before a contest. Usually, it's all 'Wilfreds turn right' and 'Mabels turn left', most places. I think they get a bit matrimonial in Streatham and Tooting in London. It was never like this at that Mecca Awards Coventry motel. What about the 7-Up winter gardens at Bradford? That Newcastle Bunny Palace, eh? That was a bit different. The mirrorball broke. The electric organ shorted the mains. And I found Doris Clovely-Rogers – you remember Doris from East Sheen – I found Doris in the band's changing-room half-clothed doing a sort of torch-tango strip in front of one of those brass Jewish candlesticks. And these bunny-girls on the floor in the black-out, chanting 'Viva España' when Doris dropped something.

AVRIL: Artie!

ARTIE: But when you get to Bexhill-on-Sea, at the Cooden Beach Peppermint lounge, if you want to share a room it's bring your marriage certificate, your passport and your mum-in-law.

[TREVIS *sits with* DOT.]

TREVIS: . . . When I said we're wed just now, I didn't just do it for that old axe, I want you to know I still do mean it. We've had our rough years –

DOT: Four of them.

TREVIS: It's been a bit left-handed and then a bit right-handed, Dot –

DOT: It's been a wank, Trevis.

TREVIS: That's not a very nice turn of phrase. It was you who kept running away. It was you who left the flat each time without a word. I can't count how many times you just deserted me like that.

DOT: Twelve.

TREVIS: I have to come and rescue you. You're on your tod. You can't rely on friends. There comes an end to the number of sofas you can find at five o'clock in the morning. Have you ever thought of leaving me at around tea-time, say?

DOT: Leaving you – is the only avenue of expression I have. You won't listen to anything else. I worked at the hospital until you decided a nurse's pay was insufficient to pay for all our lessons. Then I worked at the Co-op and we both pooled our wages for the dancing teachers and the travelling. And you decided you didn't want me as your partner anyway – you wanted Av. Now you prefer dance lessons with her. And I'm back to the girl-friend stakes.

TREVIS: I meant what I said just now – about getting married. About being married. I did.

DOT: No you didn't, darling. You just wanted me and you to have a little tidy up with our emotions, you and me, before the first dance. Sorry, Trev.

TREVIS: I'm still talking about a car. There's that maisonnette still in the back of my mind. I know a bloke who knows a bloke in Abbey National Building who is especially sympathetic to dancers.

DOT: Yes, Trev.

TREVIS: And I've proved I'm no mug when it comes to business. I discovered, it was me what did, that the manager of Barclays at Catford Cross was a retired Juvenile who'd reached bronze at waltz.

DOT: That's right –

TREVIS: I'm no mug.

DOT: That's why that milk-bill cheque you wrote didn't bounce. When it came back, it bloody rumba'd up the stairs.

TREVIS: The manager is a realist. He has said to me – 'Any time, Trev, you choose a proper job, I'll back you to the hilt.' What makes him nervous is the part-time life-style all this requires. I'm not him, Dot. I don't want to retire as a Juvenile. I don't want a bronze in a satin box in the dining-room cupboard for the rest of me life.

DOT: Trev, since when did anyone give you a bronze even, eh?
[ARTIE *is doing something with an iron and a table top where his silk corselet is laid out.*]

ARTIE: Just one word, Avril –

AVRIL: We have an agreement over contests. We avoid words.

ARTIE: One word.

AVRIL: One.

ARTIE: If you and Trevis finish in the first six, I don't want you crawling all over him. That's all. Not in front of other people from Streatham. In my walk of life I am more than likely to bump into customers, and the embarrassment is something I can do without. Remember that Amateurs' night in Dungeness in aid of the nuclear power station workers at bank holiday? It was a bit too close to the knuckle.

AVRIL: Is that what really passes through that eye-of-a-needle-sized mind of yours?

ARTIE: I've seen you pretend to like Dot just because you admire how Trev dances.

AVRIL: Well, what about Dungeness then!

ARTIE: Well, I admire how Trev dances, too. But I don't go so far as to allow him to carry me shoulder-high in a ton of taff half-way round a power station with me legs tied round his neck.

AVRIL: I don't think – long as I live – you will ever understand what is inside me. You are quite incapable of listening to the kind of questions which are wrapped deep inside me.

ARTIE: I'm quite good at answering the Christmas cracker puzzles for the kids, why don't you try me? After all, it is your old Artie here.

AVRIL: I ...

[DOT *has laid out* AVRIL's *dress in a pool shape.* AVRIL *slips out of her dressing-gown to step into the pool.*]

DOT: Av ...?

AVRIL: Thank you, Dot ... now just ...

ARTIE: Hold on.

DOT: Watch it.

ARTIE: Av ...

[ARTIE *takes command.* DOT *resists.*]

ARTIE: That's all right, Dot. I can manage.

DOT: Oh?

ARTIE: I can fasten up Avril's back just as well, ta.

AVRIL: Don't fight. Whichever one of you!

ARTIE: Now shimmer gently from the waist – up – and nobody sees your front-of-house. There.

AVRIL: Don't hurry me – I'll happily kill you if I tear –

ARTIE: Me? The number one dresser?

[DOT *turns in her dressing-gown.* TREVIS *is in his playboy shorts and sock suspenders. Shirt open and a grand chest of hair on him. He clickety-clicks and plays the matador.*]

DOT: Not in the mood just now, darling.

TREVIS: Step in.

[*She will not hurry.*]

DOT: Fancy your chances tonight, do you?

TREVIS [*helping her*]: I wasn't sat up all last night with my feet in hot vinegar for nothing.

DOT: I thought you said you sat up all night waiting for me to come home?

TREVIS: I was. I did.

DOT: And your nerves were strained rotten?

TREVIS: They were. But I thought as they were going to be strained, I might as well soften the blow by hardening up my arches, eh? And besides if you had come home early, you wouldn't have gone for steaming vinegar much, would you? Here – feel my foot.

DOT: No thanks.

TREVIS: It's gone like iron. I could knock a brick out of a wall with this foot. Solid!

DOT: I see. That really was the truth, wasn't it? A couple of corns and a slight drop in your arches, and you'll sit up all night in a cloud of wine vinegar. It had nothing to do with my absence. Takes for you to find just one bunion and I might as well not be there in your bed anyway. How long were you sat in hot vinegar?

TREVIS: All night.

[*She lifts a naked foot and grimaces at what she sees.*]

DOT: Yer daft boobie – your toe-nails have gone soft.

TREVIS: But feel me heel – it's made of iron.

[ARTIE *has pinned in the wrong place.*
AVRIL *jumps. She pulls away from him.*]

AVRIL: Finish – ow!

ARTIE: My love?

AVRIL: Finish it. Finish everything.

ARTIE [*needle in hand*]: I'm only trying –

AVRIL [*higher note*]: Why don't you stop pretending you want to do this, do that. Just finish everything once and for all! Say to me you don't really for a second want all – all this! And you hate me! And for God's sake say it! Get it over with!

ARTIE: Calm down. I don't hate you, Av. It was the needle.

AVRIL [*shaking her head*]: No . . .

ARTIE: It wasn't me . . . the needle . . .

AVRIL [*breathing deep*]: That's right . . .

ARTIE: I only want to help.

[AVRIL *screams inside and recoils.*
TREVIS *stands up.*]

TREVIS: Excuse me.

ARTIE: 'Scuse I.
  [*Eyeball to eyeball.*]
TREVIS: Yearh?
ARTIE: Oh yearh.
TREVIS: I don't like what you're doing to Av.
ARTIE: She is my wife.
TREVIS: I don't like what you're doing to your wife.
ARTIE: I merely offered to dress her as I normally do. And I consider that my right by right. So if you've –
TREVIS: I don't like what you're doing with my partner.
ARTIE: Calm down, Trev. It's me – Artie. Old friends.
TREVIS: I hope you're not trying to sabotage my dancing steps –
ARTIE: Come off it.
TREVIS: It's my money what goes into my tuition with Av. And I don't possess a lot of it. It's my all I put into Av's work-outs at the studio.
ARTIE: So do all my bonuses go to Avril. I'm helping you just as much. There's nothing in my pocket at the end of the month. You want to put your hand in my pocket to see? Eh?
TREVIS: By getting under Av's finger-nails just before we're called, I mean.
ARTIE: I try to be nice to everyone, Trev. That's my philosophy in life. But I do draw the line.
TREVIS: Oh? Where?
ARTIE: Er . . . starters . . . I don't like Dot dressing my wife.
TREVIS: Suppose your wife likes it.
ARTIE: I don't care.
TREVIS: Suppose I like it because it gives Dot something to do to get her mind off her own dance problems with you.
ARTIE: Dot and I have a very compatible combination.
TREVIS: You know what I mean.
ARTIE: I don't like to think about whatever problems you and she have. I never inquire.
TREVIS: Artie, every time we four go out on comps together, in recent times that is, an unnatural aggro gets built up.

ARTIE: It most certainly isn't me.

TREVIS: An unnatural aggro.

ARTIE: What do you call a natural one, I ask?

TREVIS: I'm thinking you are getting at Av when you know full well it puts her tempo nerves on edge. And then how can she give me maximum synchronization on the floor?

ARTIE: I don't take dancing to such serious lengths of that sort. I am a dancer. I like to dance.

TREVIS: I'm thinking that by interfering between Dot and Av when Dot wants to dress Av, you are further getting at me. Because it is just another niggle that Dot will throw back at me. And if it is not – then it is something inside you, my fine fellah, something rotten in the State of Denmark, and I don't want any of this Hamlet fine-doodle.

ARTIE: Hamlet! I don't know what Freud would say about that!

TREVIS: Don't tell him is my advice!

ARTIE: Now look –

TREVIS: I live with Dot, not you.

ARTIE: All right. You live with Dot from time to time, excuse I. But don't think I'm not aware of the fact that Av responds to you.

TREVIS: Responds?

ARTIE: Yes, responds.

TREVIS: What are you saying?

ARTIE: Out there.

TREVIS: Oh where?

ARTIE: On the floor.

TREVIS: Responds?

ARTIE: *Responds.*

TREVIS: I'll draw a veil over the fact that perhaps your natural understanding of dance is on the level which equates 4/4 time with the Eton Wall Game. But I want you to know is that I am not the same old Trev I am outside. This is a comp. I am here to get in the first six. So is Av. So before you go a step further breaking down my artistic tempo tonight – instead of putting that talcum powder round your

toes I suggest you stuff it down your patent throat. Until the
night is over.

ARTIE: That is a very unprofessional remark.

TREVIS [*raspberry*]: So is that.

ARTIE: I've always had my suspicions about the lengths you
will go to win, even when it concerns your best pal's wife.

[TREVIS *backs off.* ARTIE *fidgets with his white corselet. He
does something in his trousers with his hands to loosen himself.
He breathes in deeply. He is winded. He breathes in again.*]

ARTIE: I'd like an offer of a hand to help me fix this, please.

AVRIL: Me, me.

ARTIE: No, thanks.

AVRIL: I always do your ruddy corselet!

[ARTIE *stands stiffly.*]

DOT: I'll do it.

ARTIE: Very well.

[ARTIE *and* DOT *and* TREVIS *continue dressing.*
AVRIL *pauses at the mirror. She separates from the others.
Light on* AVRIL.]

AVRIL: . . . They used to tell us we were too young. Got wed
off too early. Then they said Artie was younger than me.
And at his stag party at the Young Rotary Club it was
nothing but – 'Who's a pretty boy being baby-snatched
then.' He was losing his hair in those days. The more he
lost the more he tried to lower the parting and sweep it
over his forehead. For a while after we had this room. And
the bed filled it. And the suitcases had to be kept outside in
the hall. In the mornings he'd wake and count the actual
number of hairs on the pillow. Some days it was fifteen.
Or twenty-two. Then he woke up and counted sixty-seven
hairs. He just cried out loud. Burst out in tears and then he
accused me of putting zinc in his food. He said it was all
zinc. Zinc in the air. Zinc in the traffic fumes. Zinc in the
fresh foods. Hardly is it, I said, you'll find zinc in me veget-
able soup – it come out of a flaming can, didn't it? And he
really got bald. It made him quite different. He wanted to
take me just as soon as any old urge got him. He had to just

do it then and there. As if time was short. Afterwards, on an evening, in the little room, his skin shone and the thinned-out hair made his eyes more lustrous, like. Gleamed in the dark, and the sweat under his chin.

... Never not having a proper place we stuck. The Council house list looked like an IBM Magna Carta already. I liked his caravan idea. And I liked his plan of going on the borrer off of his uncle. Furthermore, his uncle had this allotment patch on Denmark Hill. And we had the caravan towed through a fence opening early on a Sunday morning. Eventually the Health Authorities issued their summons. The Gas Board discovered his uncle had tapped the main to the portable cooker. So the police towed us away to a car compound. Well, we stayed in the compound for four months because we could never afford to pay what it cost to move us out. And as each week went by it got worse. We spent all our cash on Junior Sequences and Amateur Latin medallion teachers. But it became patently obvious I was so much better a dancer than Artie. He began to lose his nerve. People said – leave him. And Artie knew they did. And he felt that if we stopped partnering, we'd stop marrying an' all. When we lost some dopey little comp down in West Byfleet, one adjudicator came up to me and right in front of Artie said – if you had a better partner, you'd have got in the medals. At the station waiting for the last train, we'd lost a return ticket. And there was no money between us. Artie punched me in the mouth, and said 'Sod it!' And walked off. I had the only ticket. He hitched his way home wearing this anorak over his dancing tails. He hadn't had time to change to get the train.

... Sharon was born in the caravan. Artie started on a shoe-sales course for a chain of shops. Douglas was born nine months after Sharon, premature. We became a priority family, and the Council allowed us to buy from them with a no-down-payment scheme. It is on an estate with an attached garage which we are not allowed to rent off. Mummy gave us our little car. She drove it down and Artie put it in the garage, and she stayed a year. And there is no spare bedroom. We felt unable to control the situation because, after all, it was her Vauxhall Viva. In due course, Artie ordered mummy to leave. He wanted the sitting-room back, he said. Coincidental it may be, but that was the week the Viva failed its seventh MOT test.

. . . Sharon and Douglas live for mummy. They'd rather her than me. Every time we need to travel for comps or Amateurs Artie loads them on to mummy. Mummy wants to come back to live with us. She claims she is invaluable. Artie knows she is fifty-nine and has already had a heart attack.

. . . These years swept by me. They came like raindrops. Plonk, plonk. And gone. I couldn't tell one from the other. I realized, all of a go, that all there was left to me was a future. And it would just be the sum of everything I am now. Artie and me would continue. The kids would grow out of clothes. Mummy would get nearer and nearer. We would continue. The future would rush at us. Headlong. This is what we had agreed to. And there was no change in the pattern. Like Artie's hairs on the pillow, everything I had known or loved, things I had most sort of vividly experienced, were disappearing at great speed behind me. And that future was coming in at me closer, pouring, folding over my, living inside my lungs. Asleep at night it raced at me.

. . . I was a tiny tot in Bangor. I once climbed on board an Inter-City train which had nothing to do with me. Suddenly the doors slammed and the communicating dragon shape kicked and I fell over. How could I get off ? Don't speak to strange men. Some kind old lady help me. Never accept gifts from strangers. I asked a lady policeman where the train was going. She said – 'Chester'. There was nothing outside but cloud and grey sea all along towards Beaumaris. I pressed me nose against the window and peed into my socks.

. . . We had the kids so quick, like. This deep cold depression never left me. I was barely out of me Sharon stitches. I laid on my back and Artie took me. He would not stop. He took me as if he wanted to nail me on to the mattress. He had no idea how much it hurt. Those cries he took for

99

something else. Later, in the lavatory, I soaked the blood where the stitches had stretched. We never bought toilet rolls. I sat in the dark clutching square pads of neatly folded *Daily Mirror* until the bleeding stopped. But the pain never went. After the first child, it can hit a woman, this deep eternal depressed state. Is it like some soul thing which has been ripped out of you? And if the second kid comes too quickly on top, you never recover. You have travelled too fast with your body. The runner inside you is unable to reach the finish post. I have this sense of loss. I am cast up. And a Christmas cracker gift said once – the soul travels at the speed a camel trots ...

> [*Lights change.*
> TREVIS *and* DOT *and* ARTIE *and* AVRIL *dress together.*
> THE ORGANIZER *nips in the door. Pins a new sheet on the back. Nips out.*
> TREVIS *is curious. Looks.*]

TREVIS: Wallace and Daphne Pinkerton from Warminster! Wallace and Daphne? We smashed 'em down the Rother-hythe Tunnel Open Latins. Eh, do you remember them?

AVRIL: No. Afraid not.

TREVIS: Do go on, do. His red cummerbund came off in the samba and his trousers slipped. He's the one who was seen in the lav squeezing himself into a hernia brace. He's got this belly what sags, but in the brace he looks flat as a board. That's Wallace Pinkerton. Bloody larff!

DOT: Have you considered perhaps he does have a hernia condition? When I was in the wards in my first year, some men came in with hernias which had been left for years. They were afraid it was cancer. And they kept it from their wives. And tied themselves up like turkeys. Nothing funny about hernias.

TREVIS: You can't do Spanish with a hernia condition. You can do a sort of Hernia Spanish. But how can you grasp all the majesty of a lunge and a side kick?

DOT: Oh year? I heard of an ex-RAF fellah. Had a plastic arm and a wooden leg below the knee. He was quickstepping in local events until last year. Apparently he was apt to get a bit noisy on his pivots. But he could bowl down the prom and do a swivel on his wood peg the speed of lightning. A girl can get lifted right off both feet – he was that fast. He was called Flying Officer Woodpecker.

[TREVIS *reads off the new list on the door*.]

TREVIS: Nine-fifteen starters. Blimey, not much time left. They must be pouring in through the doors.

DOT: Oh yes, who?

TREVIS: Me fans. What's this? It says starters for the waltz. First two couples must stand by at nine o'clock. Waltz followed by foxtrot, followed by quickstep, followed by tango, then rock'n'roll, then paso doble. Long night, fellahs.

[*He and* AVRIL *make short steps in a box formation. They quickly vamp through all the items of dance. It is a display in miniature. They seem confident. Starting of course with the waltz –*]

AVRIL [*humming*]: . . .

TREVIS [*singing anything that comes into his head*]: . . .

[*They proceed through the foxtrot, quickstep, tango, rock'n'roll and paso doble.*]

TREVIS: Tango Hernia clogstep . . .

Wallace and Daph . . .

Daphne and Wal . . .

[DOT *and* ARTIE *try not to watch.* TREVIS *finds his sombrero. He and* AVRIL *glide into the paso doble.* TREVIS *is very arch on his el backs.*]

And that Spanish dressing's in me blood . . .

[DOT *covers her legs with flesh powder.* ARTIE *struggles with the reflection from his patents.*

AVRIL *and* TREVIS *stamp their feet in a dramatic Close Hold (CH) and twist on* DOT *and* ARTIE *and raise their fingers –*]

AVRIL: Clickety-click!

TREVIS: Olé!

[AVRIL *and* TREVIS *finale with a flourish.* DOT *and* ARTIE *studiedly ignore them.*

The essence of much of the sudden-change routine by AVRIL *and* TREVIS *is that most of the sequences were virtually done on the spot.*]

TREVIS [*getting nowhere*]: Olé! Olé!

[*They break away.* DOT *and* ARTIE *will not respond.* TREVIS *is silent.*

AVRIL *whisks off his sombrero and puts it on. Smiles at* TREVIS. TREVIS *goes very flat. Sullen even.*

AVRIL *grabs* TREVIS *in a cha-cha-cha basic movement. Tries to lift him. Gives his balls a tweak as they stamp out a finish.*]

AVRIL: Cough cough cough!

TREVIS [*embarrassed*]: Nah . . .

[DOT *and* ARTIE *close together on the seat.*]

ARTIE [*raising his elbow*]: Smell anything?

DOT: No.

ARTIE: It's a new one. It fights body odour under the roots of the hair. They call it 'Jungle Man'.

DOT: I can just smell it.

ARTIE: Go on.

DOT [*nose deep in his armpit*]: Sort of . . . piquant.

ARTIE: Piquant!

DOT: Sharp? Piquant?

ARTIE: Piquant, Dot, does not mean – piquant means – it's a term for describing spare ribs in a Chinese restaurant, for Christ sake!

DOT [*smelling again*]: All right. Give us your jungle again.

ARTIE: Well?

DOT: It's got a definite bark. That's it.

ARTIE [*studying his own under-arm*]: A bark? What do you think I keep under here – an alsatian dog?

DOT: I'm sorry, Artie. It's me nerves. I'm so strung up. I mean tree-bark.

ARTIE: I tell you I've got new 'Jungle Man' on and you react to it as if you've found an alsatian dog with a mouthful of old bones.

DOT: I did used to like that pine one you used.

ARTIE: Oh that was 'Essence of Scandinavia'. Pure Swedish

alpine extract. Unfortunately, it turned all my under-arm shirts bright green, and never come off in the launder-ette.

DOT [*she opens her mouth and breathes heavily all over his face*]: OK?

ARTIE: Hang about.

DOT: What!

ARTIE: What was it – fried egg?

DOT: Boiled, actually.

ARTIE: Take another one for luck.

DOT [*sucks another tablet and tries again*]: Better?

ARTIE: I used to prefer just the old chewing-gum, until you started hiding bits behind your ear-ring clip. I thought that was getting into bad habits' territory. And I must say I wasn't over-fond of the lipstick you left in the chewing-gum bits.

DOT: I tried mints, too, you know.

ARTIE: The best you ever achieved was a combination. You once had a mouthful of vanilla comforts and those kiddies' cigarettes de bonbon. Now they were lovely. We danced a fabulous Tango Serida that night and got the best points we've ever had. It was like holding a garland of flowers in me arms.

DOT: Anything else?

ARTIE [*smelling her*]: All clear.

[*He waits for her to give him a good smelling over.*]

DOT [*sniffs*]: You'll pass. Bit mouldy somewhere.

ARTIE: That's just the moth-rings the cleaners leave in me trousers.

[DOT *and* ARTIE *watch* TREVIS *and* AVRIL. *They have virtually changed sides. They sit opposite each other in their professional dancing pairings. They contemplate the new character each provides the partner with.*

ARTIE *digs deep inside himself to gain control of his competitive nerves.* AVRIL *shows them all too clearly.* DOT *seems to be in command, just.*

They begin to look doll-like. Here is TREVIS *trying his tails. There is* ARTIE *brushing his white waistcoat.* AVRIL *and*

DOT *fuss over their shoes. They bend them over and spit into them, and try to rub grime off the soles.*]

TREVIS [*to* AVRIL]: Me first teacher said before you go out you have to be clean. You have to feel clean. Deep inside. I had a bath in salts. I kept me feet up all night in vinegar. Under the ole pits I've got a gallon of 'Male Leather No. 1'. Spray gargle for the verbals. Talc in the crutch, odour-eating pads in me footsies, 'Olives of Viburnum' on me flowing locks, and I'm anybody's.

AVRIL: I warned you about buying that Viburnum at the shop. There is no such thing as a Viburnum tree.

TREVIS [*picks up a bottle and reads it*]: This ancient Himalayan tree has not been seen in Europe for hundreds of years. These rare olives produce a musky tang reminding you of cherry trees swaying in the snow-covered pasture.

AVRIL: I don't care what you say – there is no such tree as a Viburnum. You've been done.

TREVIS: I can just see this tree in me mind's eye, out there swaying.

AVRIL [*sniffing*]: And frankly it smells like goat and parsley sauce.

TREVIS: Its lacquer gives that extra allure. That's all.

ARTIE: It's all right, Trev, we know how well you can dance, you don't need any beautific concoctions to improve you. Or Av.

TREVIS: Do I detect a faint hint of old grapes already?

ARTIE [*gently but steaming*]: You don't need to tango up to me with your clickety-clicks. And I don't think Av needs to grasp your bollocks in a friendly twosome to keep you on your toes for the comp.

TREVIS: Oh yearh? Fear and trembling is it that things may not go too well for Artie tonight? On the floor? With Dot?

DOT [*holds* ARTIE'*s arm*]: No, it isn't. Artie is trying to prepare himself for our chances. And so am I. We may not be in your class, but we have to compose ourselves.

AVRIL: Trev's joking, Artie. Honest.

ARTIE: Trev never jokes when he's in his patents.

DOT [*to* ARTIE]: Calm down. Come on.

ARTIE: I'm being deliberately ruffled, when I'm requiring peak attention to my own chances.

TREVIS: Ruffled! How can you ruffle a duck's egg?

ARTIE: Simple. By taking it out of its nest!

[*He snatches at* TREVIS's *hair. The wig comes off.*
ARTIE *clucks and waves it around.*
TREVIS *goes for him.*]

TREVIS: Now!

ARTIE [*chickening it*]: ...

TREVIS: Those feathers aren't cheap!

ARTIE [*birding it*]: Oh, cheep cheep!

[AVRIL *tries to break the men up.* ARTIE *falls back on a chair. She rolls on top of him with her legs in the air to reach the wig.*
DOT *scrambles. The dresses are very bulky.*
ARTIE *disappears under* AVRIL's *skirts.*
TREVIS *ends up on the floor with* DOT *astride his neck.*
GERRY *opens the door.*]

GERRY: ... 'Allo! ... what's this, then? ... The dirt track scrambler gavotte, is it? Or a new waltz courtesy of Cardiff Arms Rugby Stadium?

[*The* COUPLES *climb up from the floor.* AVRIL *gets the toupé back on to* TREVIS's *head. It looks none too secure.*]

GERRY: I hate to interfere with yer all-in wrestling. But I need yer biogs for me patter.

[*The* COUPLES *resume places in the dressing-room.*]

GERRY: Now, we have Avril and Artie Vickers. And we have Dot and Trevis Comport. Neither couple dance in any other event tonight but the local district comp. You are all at the bottom of the ladder looking up at the stars.

TREVIS: Oh true. You can put it, can't you? Oh it's straight poetry tonight from William Alfred Longfellow, init?

GERRY: But neither couples dances as partners on the floor. We have therefore Avril – ?

AVRIL: Who dances with Trevis.

GERRY: And Artie – ?

DOT: I dance with Artie.

GERRY: Remind me, dear, we are – ?

DOT: Dorothy Dooly, please. I like to use my maiden name.

GERRY: Trevis, what do you do, love?

TREVIS: I can feel me fist knuckling over –

GERRY: Silly me – Brockwell Park Baths, wasn't it? I was more concerned in what you did during the winter months?

TREVIS: Watch it!

GERRY: What do you do with your muscles between winter and spring?

TREVIS: I'll bloody do you, tinkerbelle, half a chance mate!

GERRY: Now, now. There's that little twinkle again.

[TREVIS *is snarling and curling back his top lip until the white teeth show.*

AVRIL *tenderly straightens his toupé for him.*]

AVRIL: Button up, Trev. There's some chest hair showing.

TREVIS: Whose side you on?

AVRIL [*to* GERRY]: Trev's got a thoroughbred way with him. You have to handle with care.

GERRY: Trevis?

TREVIS [*pulling himself together, unruffling the artistic edges*]: I . . . do part-time in the kiddies' zoo . . . I . . . look after the white rabbits and the fluffy Peking bantams, and if there is one word about –

GERRY: The fluffy ones are the rare breed ones with feathers all around their little toes, am I right?

TREVIS [*going through the roof*]: I'm not taking any more! My rag's flying high!

[AVRIL *clutches on to tempestuous* TREVIS. *He is bursting at the seams now.*]

GERRY: I was only interested.

TREVIS: Oh no!

GERRY: I have to have me little questions.

TREVIS [*steaming*]: Oh yes!

GERRY: We are tempestuous.

TREVIS: Oh yearh?

[AVRIL *persuades* TREVIS *to sit down.* TREVIS *is shaking. She sits on him to keep him on the chair. His toupé wobbles.*]

GERRY: Now, Artie, what do you get up to when you're not

loafing around gents' cottages in the Underground stations on a Saturday night?

ARTIE: Eh?

GERRY: You do something novel for a living?

ARTIE: I am a shoe manager at H. W. Goldings, Streatham High Street. Big chain. Many prospects. And I don't hang around cottages on the Underground.

GERRY: You put the customers' toes into the shoes with those shoe-horns?

ARTIE: It's a bit more complicated than that, yes.

GERRY: How long have you been married, Artie?

ARTIE: Eight years.

GERRY: You are happily married? Very happily married? Or over the moon with love for Avril?

ARTIE: I-am-over-the-moon.

GERRY: And how do you feel, Avril?

ARTIE: I've just told you how she feels.

GERRY: I like to hear the wifey's side of the tale.

AVRIL [*dull stare*]: I am also over the moon.

GERRY: Can I say it has been the happiest years of your life?

ARTIE: You can.

AVRIL: If you like.

GERRY: Now er . . . Trev and Dot, where did you spend your honeymoon?

TREVIS: On me father's mobile home at Dungeness.

GERRY: You like a sea-view? Through the panoramic window?

TREVIS: The panoramic window does not face the sea. It faces a big hole in the cliff which was once a flint works.

GERRY: It must have been rather crowded in there with your father as well?

TREVIS: No, not at all. I bought him a crate of beer and lent him my motorbike for the weekend and told him to sod off and not come back till ten o'clock Monday morning.

GERRY: Dot is happily married and you look forward to what?

TREVIS: She looks forward to having two big kids, which we've always wanted, and the day when we can persuade a mortgage company to lend us seven thousand quid for this flat we've seen by Catford Dog Stadium.

GERRY: I was asking Dot.

DOT: He's just told you.

GERRY: Don't you have an extra little word you'd like to add, Dot?

DOT: No.

GERRY: How many kids you got, Avril?

AVRIL: Three.

ARTIE: Two.

GERRY: Hallo. Someone's counted wrong.

AVRIL: Three. Sharon is seven. Douglas is six. And Artie is thirty-two.

GERRY: Why, Dot, do you want to be a local district dance champion?

DOT: Because – I do not like washing dishes or scrubbing Y-fronts, and because putting on fancy clothes gives me an unusual sexy buzz. And anything is better than the sheer drudgery of a woman's domestic lot. That do?

GERRY: No dear. It's a glamorous answer I'm seeking. You have always admired Elizabeth Taylor's hair-styles. Or you have a missionary zeal to teach the tango in south-east Asia to a great Prince of Bangkok. Avril?

AVRIL: I dance because it is something I am much better at than my husband. And it gives me a sense of control. Yes?

GERRY: No. Sorry I asked.

[GERRY *hesitates in his stride.*]

. . . Has any one of you got an unusual story you'd like me to tell my audience?

AVRIL: Well, when I became pregnant again, four weeks and four days after giving birth to my first child, I was so depressed I took two overdoses of Mogadon. I also bought a secondhand cut-throat razor. I sharpened it with olive oil on the kitchen step. But I never used it. Courage really. The sight of anyone's blood actually does me in. I throw up.

GERRY: Anybody else got a hobby my audience is dying to hear about? I was thinking more on the lines of shubunkin goldfish or homing pigeons which have broken long-distance records.

DOT: I like sex.

TREVIS: Oh yearh?

DOT: I like sex. It's an unusual thing for a woman to say. But I like to have two orgasms in a night's whatsit. I like a bit at the start. And then I find I can go for a bigger bit towards the end. In the middle I get rather tired. But I build up to it like a finale. And I haven't had anything like that for bloody months. Do you want to know why?

GERRY: I don't think my –

TREVIS: Thank you, Dot. Thank you. That was just what my doctor ordered. I'm glad you brought that up. It helps me to keep my confidence for the dances no end. Thank you, Dot.

[TREVIS *breathes in deeply and hangs on to his artificial satin revers.*]

GERRY: Just remains for me to say Lord Luck go with the winners tonight.

TREVIS: Hasn't Artie asked to see the booby prize?

DOT: No he hasn't.

TREVIS: Go on, Artie – tell him you'd like to see the army boot with the half-bottle of rat's piss in it!

GERRY: It is a non-alcoholic bubbly-type wine.

TREVIS: Artie wants a gander. He's got a fine chance for that.

GERRY [*as* ARTIE *climbs out of his chair*]: All runners-up will share in the medals. We have enough specially engraved medallions to go round. Last word though – the actual two winners cannot leave the premises with the award cups. The top cup has to go back to the Barclays Bank vault in Tooting Bec Avenue. But the lucky outright winner will get an identical copy delivered by hand within a fortnight. The cup will be made of a uniquely devised engineering process. It will be of a high quality silver-finish art-deco hand-polished –

TREVIS: Tin.

GERRY: We call it Prestige Ware. The smaller cup can be

taken home on the night. Bronze-effect inside, silver-effect outside with pear-drop handles –

TREVIS: Still tin.

GERRY: Knickers!

[GERRY *bangs the door and exits.*

ARTIE *walks across to the tannoy speaker on the wall in the dressing-room. He switches it on.* VOICES *and the sound of a* BAND *tuning up come through the machine.*

We hear –]

ORGANIZER's VOICE [*she appears to be clattering along the corridor from door to door*]: . . . Couples number one and two, will you please go and stand under the arcade curtains now. There will not be a second call . . . Couples three and four, I want you out of the rooms and on the corridor now . . . couples five and six will get a knock and then a shout and I'll not repeat myself . . . All artistes to stand ready for first call . . .

[TREVIS *goes across to the tannoy. Switches it off.* ARTIE *stands up.*

In the sudden quiet, ARTIE *is sitting beside* AVRIL, *and* TREVIS *has to go back to sit with* DOT. ARTIE *has virtually forced their coupling arrangements back into the private arena.*]

ARTIE: . . . Douglas wants roller skates. Now Sharon wants that roller board dangerous thing. Then he'll want a six-gear speed bike – Japanese. And she'll start pinching her nipples to see if they'll stand up in the air. Then Douglas will be three inches taller than me, and I don't know what to say to him now. I've never seen mathematics done his way before. In my youth it was those good chestnuts like that one about the man who walked into a wireless shop with a five-pound note. The wireless cost thirteen shillings and four pence, two ten-bob notes fell on the floor, and so where was the missing six bob and eight pence? Or something like that. I could always crib that from my deskmate Four Eyes Etchingham. When I look at Douglas's sums today – I'd need a calculator.

AVRIL: I think you make a very good father, Artie. Far better than me as a mum. You actually care for them. You make sure Sharon does her American ballet. And you walk Douglas all the way to tap classes and wait for him to finish. You don't fight them like I do.

ARTIE: I think about the little bleeders night and day, don't you?

AVRIL: No.

ARTIE: I know I never turned out to look the image of your father. I never really ever possessed that je ne sais quois which gives that added ring of zest to achievement. And I know you could have married better.

AVRIL: No, Artie.

ARTIE: No. I understand. I mean I would have been a better man at many things if . . . I was always too astonished, I think. It amazed me when boys at school were on motorbikes all of a sudden. Then one day, when we were most broke – you remember – I was walking down the Common and I saw that unpleasant rat's fart E. J. Fotheringay, Form 3C, driving a brand-new Ford Galaxy with a sliding roof! Fotheringay was that little nark who stole the school firework funds. So we stripped him in the bog and shoved an entire Cluster Star Thunderer rocket right up his fundamental. Fotheringay! Blimey! At our wedding your family bought you the white dress. That old blue suit I had was Grandad Eddie's from when he got wed in the blitz. That's why it had those thick turn-ups with old halfpenny coins in them.

AVRIL: Don't . . . please . . .

ARTIE: I mean I never do much rabbiting on because I don't really want to know the answers, do I? I don't really ever ask what is in your mind, eh? Just don't. I like to think of it as it was in the beginning. Tooting Bec Common and the gymnastics we got up to on that bench behind the dog pound – Night after night even in the rain – bloody ace that was. Bench seat was only two feet wide. I remember that brass plaque it had on the back – 'This bench is a gift from the late Alderman Arther Simpson Sackhurst for the well-being of the community.' There'd be a difference of opinion on the exact meaning of 'well-being' between the old Alderman and me, eh? That shoe manufacturers' weekend in a Scottish golfing hotel – that was swank, wan' it? A joke really. Neither of us could play golf. Me – I never dared to learn. And I've got a coupla polyphoto sheets of you very hazy and wobbly in a booth on Argyll platform, when we missed the sleeper back. But in them you are still actually smiling, you know – smiling/laughing/smiling/laughing. I liked you that way. It was as if you intended to battle through all adversities in life with me. I kept everything. Those snaps when you seemed to smile through thunder clouds. Every bus ticket we shared. Every cinema slip. Every Saturday afternoon dance lesson receipt. Kept the lost property ticket at Charing Cross after I lost your brolly for you, and even after I got it back, I kept it. It was your favourite retractable brolly. I even tried to nick that park bench belonging to the Alderman fellah and put it outside the caravan on Uncle's cabbage allotment.

[AVRIL *places her hands on her face and rocks back and forth.*

Her shoulders shake.]

. . . nah don't do that . . . don't be that way, Av . . . you'll ruin that hair-do. And I can't put back the pieces like you can.

[*A pause then –*

DOT *and* TREVIS *move a fraction.* DOT *wants more space for the flounced-out back of her skirts which rise up above her shoulders as she sits.*]

TREVIS: I don't want to labour it – but as long as I've known you I don't think you have ever heard me use the word 'orgasm' in front of a total stranger like that.

DOT: What orgasm?

TREVIS: Your twice nightly, once before and once after, with, I suppose, a pistachio ice cornet on top for in-betweens.

DOT: Oh – orgasms. Well?

TREVIS: I find that a private matter between us.

DOT: I thought it was a fast way of getting rid of that little tit.

TREVIS: Don't tell a lie, Dot.

DOT: I thought you didn't like him?

TREVIS: You knew it would humiliate me, that was it.

DOT: I'm sorry, darling – it was the truth.

TREVIS: Truth, like caviar or egg and bacon and mushrooms, is kept for special occasions.

DOT: Go on, you big stiff. How could that hurt? You're that vain it'd take a Black and Decker drill to get to you.

TREVIS: You hurt, mate. Not just me artiste's tempo either. You hurt.

DOT: No. What got under your skirt was that –

TREVIS: I wish you wouldn't refer to me as someone who goes around wearing skirts!

DOT: Got under your goat then – was that piece of rubbish fancied you something rotten.

TREVIS: He's married. He's a grown-up married old man.

DOT: Fancied you, Trev.

TREVIS: You heard that old trout – the two of them are married. He just talks that way. That's how they used to be in Jack Buchanan's day.

DOT: Oh yes he did. Like hot mustard.

TREVIS: You don't understand – in their day they talked and ballroom-danced like that – it was a way of having class.

DOT: What was it? Make a mistake in the swimming pool last summer? Give him the accidental eye, did you? It's vanity, Trev, it'll see you down no end of queer street.

TREVIS: It's not like that any more, love. It's a different world. A bloke can cover himself in Viburnum Tree olive oil and nobody's going to wince. A man is allowed to wear undershorts like me orange satin playboy shorts with the 'come and get it' writing on the front. You gotta be macho loose in these days. Your electricity has gotta stand out. You walk down the street and they all turn round and look at you and the fur on the back of your head stands up with a tickle: that's macho man. So . . . just because I wear a toupé . . . ride a 350cc bike . . . like black leather plastic gear . . . wear studs . . . and I collect show biz pics of Judy Garland, it does not mean I'm a left-handed five-shilling pound note.

DOT: I see.

TREVIS: When I wooed you you was in the last year of the nursing finals. Just before you qualified for ward-work full-time. I didn't take you down the pub, pour three pints of brown ale down you and get the bus to the local fish-and-chips. The first time I peeled off in the daylight in front of you. You on the bed. I wasn't wearing old Y-fronts with the Sunlight laundry tag still stuck on. Remember? I ordered you two white rum cocktails. We went to the Imperial Ballroom to watch Glennice and Gaynor do exhibitions. When we got back, I pulled down me trousers and what did you behold?

DOT: I don't know. I've forgotten. What?

TREVIS: Italian racing blue satin playboy shorts with maroon stripes. That's what. Playboy macho I'm talking about.

DOT: Oh, is that what it was.

[TREVIS *is suddenly diving into his gear laid out on a table. He has lost something.*]

TREVIS: . . . Dot? Did I pack me Muhammad Ali medallion for the paso doble?

[*She shrugs. He dives into his Spanish costume which hangs on the wall beside other jackets.*]

. . . I put it in the top inside pocket with the Violet breath lozzies.

DOT: Don't look at me, sweety.

[THE ORGANIZER *pops her head around the door.*]

ORGANIZER: Couple number six by the arcade curtain. Couple number six by the arcade curtain. Thank you. I won't say it twice.

[*She vanishes.*

ARTIE *and* DOT *stand up.* ARTIE *has pinned his number* '9' *on.*

AVRIL *and* TREVIS *also stand. He has his number* '6' *on. They stand before the mirrors. A last look. The final touch. Their Spanish costumes and dresses, their rock'n'roll jackets,*

114

their sombrero hats and castanets, their mounds of shoes,
shirts, make-up and hair-pieces are around them.
ARTIE *and* AVRIL *and* DOT *kiss or touch each other,*
gestures of goodwill. And nerves. TREVIS *turns up the tannoy.*
We hear applause from the audience.]

ARTIE: Good luck, Av.
AVRIL: Good luck, Dot.
DOT: You too, Av.
ARTIE: Smash 'em, Dot, eh?

[DOT *helps fan out* AVRIL's *taffeta swan-shaped layers.*
Pools of swaying material.
TREVIS *cannot leave his mirror. He dusts down and brushes*
up.]

AVRIL: And Artie. Honest. Genuine.

[ARTIE *cracks a grin.*]

TREVIS [*at his bow-tie*]: Thanks, fellahs. I need it.

[*The applause continues from the tannoy.*]

end of act one

ACT TWO

SCENE ONE

[*Lights on the podium corner.* GERRY *holds his mike.*
The rest of the ballroom area is in darkness.]

GERRY: Now here we have couple number six, Trevis Comport
and Avril Vickers. Trevis is a part-time swimming instructor. When the lovely girls he coaches give him a moment off
he likes to look after white rabbits and fluffy-footed foreign
bantams. Avril is a very happily married housewife. She
likes always to be in control of her domestic chores, and is
keen on messing about on the kitchen step sharpening
cutlery to get her mind off life's little wrinkles.

[*The* BAND *strikes up in a waltz.*
A spotlight picks up TREVIS *and* AVRIL. *They step out.*
*They dance across the floor. They select their own movements
to inset the dialogue. There are a number of movements
which can provide the space for the words, i.e. – the Drag
Hesitation (DH) and the Hesitation Change (HC) and
the Open Impetus Turn (OIT) provide pause-effects.
Otherwise, it is best to seek the word within the tempo.*]

AVRIL: . . . How are you feeling, Trev?

TREVIS: . . . Don't talk.

AVRIL: . . . You smell nice.

TREVIS: . . . Feeling fine.

AVRIL: . . . Dear Trev.

TREVIS: . . . 'Scuse I.

AVRIL: . . . I wanted to tell you something in private.

TREVIS: . . . Well, you can't get more private than this.

AVRIL: . . . I'm glad you feel well, Trev.

TREVIS: . . . We're in with a chance, mate.

AVRIL: . . . You seem so confident, Trev.

TREVIS: . . . What's the matter, don't you trust me?

AVRIL: . . . I –

TREVIS: . . . Yearh?

AVRIL: . . . I just don't want to upset your tempo.

TREVIS: ... Try me – tonight I'm a tiger.

[*A Drag Hesitation (?)*]

AVRIL: ... It's Dot.

TREVIS: ... It is?

AVRIL ... She's asked me to tell you –

TREVIS: ... She has?

[*He is slightly uncertain as he is doing his best to concentrate on their combination. Element of abstraction in his mind.*]

AVRIL: ... Now I don't want you to spin me too hard.

TREVIS: ... Do I ever?

AVRIL: ... When I tell you what I have to –

TREVIS: ... Ay wot?

AVRIL: ... And don't lose your step.

TREVIS: ... Me? The expert! It would take a force ten gale to upset me sway.

AVRIL: ... Dot –

TREVIS: ... Yes – Dot?

AVRIL: ... Is going to leave you tonight and she is never ever going to come back.

[*They dance on. And finish another bar. They complete the dance to the* BAND *back up front, or down stage to the audience.*

They sway into an elegant finale. TREVIS *leans back, chin up. Bogus grimace, half a grin.* AVRIL *maintains a fine Lily of the Valley pose. Lights catch the lustre in her hair, the allure of her face sequins and the flouncing pool of her taffeta. Stars scatter in the gods.*]

AVRIL [*big smile*]: ... That was the worst sway you've ever done to me.

TREVIS [*gritting his teeth under the stars*]: I'm not bloody surprised.

[*Lights on the dancers snap shut.*

Darkness. A pause, then –

Lights on the dressing-room. DOT *and* ARTIE *quietly go about their final toilet before their call.*

THE ORGANIZER *stands in the dressing-room. But* DOT *and* ARTIE *do not seem to hear.* THE ORGANIZER *does address them at times, at other times, she speaks to us.*]

DOT *still concentrates on the sponge with the leg-tan colouring on her thighs. With care.*]

ORGANIZER: Yes, I met Mr Hawking during an unusual part of the war. I always call him Mr Hawking. And during comps when we officiate, he makes a habit of referring to me as the Organizer. Other people marvel at his self-control. Like that he is, my Mr Hawking.

I had been wed before to a brute. Oh a brute. He was a grand-looker with these large biceps, and he worked the Suffolk cart-horses for Watkins Brewery. I thought I was in love. At night he talked about money and beer. He had these huge hands and muscles. Stripped down in the sunshine on Southport beach he was quite a tonic. But in bed, after the talk, when he dipped the kerosene lamp, I shuddered. His hands took hold of me and bludgeoned me on the pillow. His knees on me bosoms and his weight as he whacked my head and my shoulders with these half-closed hands like axes. He waited until I stopped screaming. Then he casually drifted down me body and took me. Afterwards, I rolled up on the wicker chair with a blanket by the window. Sobbing me eyes out, trying not to touch these black bruisings on my upper body. Praying there was no blood. I dared not move an inch. Wicker-work crackles like gunfire. I dared not have him wake. I curled up frozen stiff. And the draught blew the acrid fume from the kerosene wick which still glowed. The smell was bitter. Burned-out cotton and oil in the nostrils. I wouldn't sneeze, would I? Oh, never.

. . . At the outbreak of war, the Brute, I call him the Brute, was out there in the first big retreat of the French and the British. The Brute was always declared 'missing' but never 'Missing believed dead'. It was in order to give me hope. I began work as a counter-girl in the cologne-spray department of Debenham and Freebody's. At night I was a voluntary air-raid warden. On Saturday evenings, we girls would hang around the Coronet bar in the Cumberland Hotel, Marble Arch, to try to meet the Canadian boys. If we were lucky, we'd all march arm in arm down to Eros and the Canadians would take us into the Café de Paris. We drank

White Ladies and I slipped all the maraschino cherries I could steal into my handbag. I needed them for my angel cakes which I loved to cook. And I danced all night with a gentle Canadian pilot called Armand, to the music of 'Snake-hips Johnson' and his band. Some beez-neez in the Women's Voluntary Service discovered we shopgirls liked to stay the night in the cellars of big stores like Debenham's, especially if Adolf hunned all night long with his bombs. So it was decided to provide an Events Officer for us girls. Along came my Mr Hawking. He was Gerry then. I called him Gerry in those days. Gerry was a civilian, and none of us queried just why he was not out there in Europe with the other lads. Gerry had been organizing dances for RAF Wakefield, and had introduced Modern Ballroom Dancing up there. As soon as he found all us girls in the basements of these big London stores he got to work in no time. He got us girls dancing as partners, and there we were, in the blitz, in those giant stores' basements, dancing Amateur Latins to a pile of 78s by Xavier Cugat and his Waldorf-Astorians. Mr Hawking organized the comps. We girls just went along. My team was, of course, the Debenham and Freebody's All Girl Stompers. And our first basement comp was against Sears and Wells' Horseladies of the Apocalypse. They had an unfair advantage. We beat the Harrods' Maxixe Maidens, and we absolutely crushed the Bourne and Hollingsworth Hokey-Pokeys. What a whirl it all was. One night I was jitterbugging – I had lost my handbag – with a bra-cup full of glacé cherries. The next I was competing against Pontings' Red Hot Peppers, in Lillywhites' tennis basement. In between dances, I used to stand by the lift shaft and listen to the boom-boom of the night sky. I thought of the Brute, and shivered.

... Gerry was the one. I kissed and hugged Armand goodbye at Waterloo. But when Gerry suddenly vanished from among us, I felt a deep hurt. I yearned to hear his delicate MBD drill. Then a girl at Derry and Toms told me he was in a prison camp outside Warwick. When I visited him there he collapsed in front of me. He was so grateful that just one of us girls had bothered to find him. He said he was inside as a conscientious objector. He begged me to come back. I took a job as a land-girl not ten miles away. I visited him every Saturday morning, until war ended.

[*Lights change. The dressing-room fades to black. On the podium corner,* GERRY *stands with his mike. He is bathed in the spangly colours the* BAND *might play under. For the moment the rest of the ballroom area is dark.*]

GERRY: We have, boys and girls, couple number nine! Artie Vickers and Dorothy Dooly. Artie is a branch manager of a shoe shop, and his hobby is visiting the old cottages of England. Dorothy is a charming young newly-wed who is saving for a home in the direction of Dulwich. She likes theatre, and goes to shows which feature cheerful bedroom romps. And she prefers to use her maiden name when she's on the floor.

[*The spotlight floods down on* ARTIE *and* DOT *as they glide forward into the waltz.*]

DOT: ... I'm not going to beat about the bush.

ARTIE: ... Should hope not ... this isn't a pony trek.

DOT: ... Artie?

ARTIE: ... It's strict tempo.

DOT: ... I want you to prepare yourself for a shock.

ARTIE: ... What, right now?

DOT: ... Yes.

ARTIE: ... In the middle of me waltz?

DOT: ... Yes.

ARTIE: ... Oh God. I think I've guessed.

DOT: ... Oh, clever you are.

ARTIE: ... You've got cramp?

DOT: ... No I haven't.

ARTIE: ... Yer non-skid's come off yer sole?

DOT: ... No.

ARTIE: ... You've got your monthly?

DOT: ... Daft bugger.

ARTIE: ... You're in the bun trade and we can't dance no more?

DOT: ... Don't you ever see anything in a different light?

ARTIE: ... I give up. Surprise me.

DOT: ... Avril.

ARTIE: ... – My wife –

DOT: ... Avril has decided to leave you for ever.

[*His face falls off. They dance away.*]

ARTIE: ... Eh?

DOT: ... You heard.

ARTIE: ... When?

DOT: ... Tonight.

[*The ballroom area darkens as they dance away from us and the music fades. Above us the stars in the ceiling wink less.*

Lights on the dressing-room. AVRIL *tries to cool herself down.* TREVIS *kicks his patents off and pours talcum powder in them.*

GERRY *stands in the dressing-room. He gets the odd glance from* TREVIS *or* AVRIL. *Mostly he addresses the past which speeds up to him, overtakes him, and carries him up withal.*]

GERRY: I had made up my mind I would leave boys alone until after mum and dad died. I could live with the thought of them looking on from high, but not with the risk they might discover my inclination whilst they were among the living. But I always counterbalanced this feeling with the belief that really I was quite normal. That at the most extreme I was bi-sexual. I didn't have anything to do with those collective wanks the boys in the second cricket eleven got up to under the bicycle sheds. Boys with their heads leaning against the wall panting, and each one in line pulling off the other. It seemed more like a car assembly line in Dagenham to me. After school, I worked like a maniac at the opposite sex. I spent more time and thought and ingenuity in extracting large lumps of flesh from brassières and kneading them with my fingertips than I dare recall. I developed another theory that I had an abiding passion for legs in sheer seam stockings. A girl called Ivy allowed me the freedom of her knickers and a twenty-minute half-time to unclasp her bottle-green suspender belt. It was all achieved during an emergency black-out on Streatham High Street in the milkbar opposite the Dance Locarno. We could hear the crump of a bomb over Croydon way. It was the 'Moo Cow Milk Bar' all Junior dancers used. I did get my fingers inside Ivy's knickers, and it was very wet, and I withdrew them with a sense of surprise. No, it was terror, really. I felt she was demanding too much of me. I was a very young twenty-five.

. . . Frederick – we called him Freddie behind his back but he insisted on his full monicker splendificus during Junior comps – Frederick had bold ginger hair and a pale thin body covered with a blaze of freckles. We hid from our awful partners inside the gents' lav. I shared a cubicle with him. We both got out our dicks to pee together. But our dicks insisted on standing up, thus making the passing of water a splashy affair. In the end we rubbed our dickies together and we serviced one another with a simultaneous whoosit. It was so intense and perfect an eruption. A culmination of all our glances across the floor. I don't know what the adjudicator would have thought – two grown boys in white ties and tails and patents, flies unbuttoned, Y-fronts down, J. Arthur Ránking the night away over a lavatory seat. Frederick loved Italian restaurants in Soho. In comps he disguised the garlic with mouthfuls of aniseed. But I forgave Frederick most things. Later he danced tap for the Squadronnaires' chorus line. He became Petty Officer Shenanigens on a South African ship – Durban to Montevideo. He wrote me a cheerful postcard inviting me to stay in a hotel with him in Montevideo. I was not prepared to go that far.

. . . Mum and dad didn't die. I was involved in an incident in room 213 of the Cumberland Hotel. The lounge waitress used her door key and found four members of the Royal Canadian Air Force Jitterbug Team in the shower-bath. And me. It might have gained an inch of propriety if I'd drawn the pink shower curtain. As Events Officer for the WVS I was court-martialled and interned for twenty-four months at Warwick gaol. There was a ruling about corrupting allies during war-time. It was all at the pleasure of King George VI, and I just sighed. If only he knew. Mum and Dad didn't. I proposed instant marriage to this friendly girl who came up to visit me. She used to dance in one of those store dance teams I put together. I told her I was inside because I was a conscientious objector. And the authorities had discovered a letter of mine. I had written to the League of Nations Human Rights Committee, Dublin. Liar.

. . . My wife liked sequence dancing, and the Lindy Hop. She brought me angel cakes topped with maraschino cherries every Saturday morning. On release, I swore never to look at another boy with freckles or a Canadian accent ever again. The law was too strong. It was all right for a few in Eaton Square. I was made to feel sordid. I was a leper in a house of whores. Mind you, it was quite an art to disguise things then. If you had as much as called me a nancy-boy, I'd have bridled.

. . . On our first anniversary, we moved back to London. With absolute fear and trembling I visited a certain notorious Turkish bath. There was a steam-room at the back. I took my little towel and glass of water and crept in. It was all so dense and white, my elbow couldn't see my knee. All around on the benches sat quiet stony figures. We were waiting but nobody would make the first move. But nothing happened. Bodies alone. Aching eyes. I took it for so long. I couldn't tell hot sweat from tears on my cheeks. Drops of water hung on my ear-lobes, heavy, perfect and precarious. Later, I learned there was a police raid only the week before.

. . . I would never stand for bottoms-up intercourse. A bit of touching, yes, nothing more. You get afraid of what you might become. See it in others. The way the past is never behind you. It is there, up ahead, racing towards you breathless for a collision. I saw the old men on overgrown bomb-sites up Denmark Hill. They'd stand in the bushes waiting for the schoolboys. That indecent haste to show themselves. A sly wink and a beckon to a boy with a satchel and round cap. And old yellow knuckles gripping a chunk of cottonwool in readiness.

. . . My wife had done away with the sexual act. Her first husband was known as the Brute. She liked her hot bath, and me to stroke her shoulders and her neck and her upper-arms with gentle fingers. I put olive oil on her arms and rubbed her there. She'd whimper in the dark as if I was rubbing away dreadful wounds. She liked an old wicker chair by the window. She undressed and laid her clothes on that chair. We had a special joke on those days. She said to me, 'What if the Brute comes back? You'd be a bigamist, Gerry!' Me? A bigamist; I thought – at last, I'd found a role in life. I was someone at last. I felt like I'd been handed a George Medal. And Mum and dad had not yet died.

[*Lights change in the dressing-room.* ARTIE *and* DOT *pile in. And* GERRY *discreetly steps outside.*]

TREVIS: Hey, Artie, did you time me number? It felt like two minutes.

ARTIE: No I did not.

TREVIS: You gotta watch out for that spot. If you hesitate before you go into finale spin, the spot will move away. It's directed by an idiot. I want to talk to you about something after these dances are done.

ARTIE: It's all right, Trev. We don't have to wait until then. You don't need the results announced so you can bolster up your confidence. You can share your little secret with me now.

TREVIS: Eh?

ARTIE: One thing I will say about meself, I can face facts when they're staring me in my face.

TREVIS: Are you trying to upset my tempo, is that what all this malarcky is about?

ARTIE: Go on, man, you can tell me straight. I'm the one most interested, on whom your little dirty secret most reflects.

TREVIS: I'm not in the mood for musical chairs games. And

frankly, right now, I don't give a clog dance on a bed of nails what most reflects on you at all!

ARTIE: You want my wife? Take her!

TREVIS: Eh?

ARTIE: You want my mother-in-law?

TREVIS: Not to my knowledge, no.

ARTIE: My low-cost mortgage with a ten-year extension?

TREVIS: No.

ARTIE: That car of mine which don't ever work and the RAC Rescue Service has put a ban on? Go on.

TREVIS: Artie –

ARTIE: Want to try starting it every morning on a road without a slope? Like to take my kids to school each morning? Here yeh're! He're the keys!

TREVIS: I appreciate the joke on Trevis. I'm sure you've all planned it nice –

ARTIE: In future kindly have the grace to come up to me and ask me if you can ten years of my life take without as much as a beg yours big toe!

TREVIS: I already have your wife.

ARTIE: Don't I just know!

TREVIS: Avril's me partner, right?

ARTIE: Oh, so right.

TREVIS: I don't know what tricks you're all up to, but I'll not be interfered with.

ARTIE: Oh, nice one, that!

[ARTIE *cannot keep still. The door opens.* THE ORGANIZER *pops her head round –*]

ORGANIZER: Couple number six, are you going to foxtrot or aren't you?

[TREVIS *grabs* AVRIL *and leads her out.*]

TREVIS: I certainly am!

[THE ORGANIZER *stands firm. The door shuts.*
The dressing-room darkens.
Lights on the arcade curtains, as TREVIS *and* AVRIL *straighten themselves up to prepare to step out. It is not a spotlight. It is a more abstract effect.* TREVIS *and* AVRIL

step into position. And as the BAND *strikes up, they trot
forward on to the ballroom area and pose with arms wide.
The* BAND *gives them a big intro. Tympanum fanfare.
Lights black immediately on* TREVIS *and* AVRIL.
The BAND *stops.
Lights in the dressing-room.* ARTIE *and* DOT *continue with
their toilet.* THE ORGANIZER *is still.*]

ORGANIZER: Mr Hawking, with his good reputation for
dance tuition, became an accredited instructor with the
Imperial Society of Teachers of Dancing. Mr Hawking
hired a nissen hut backing on to Tooting Bec Common,
and we called it the Gerald Hawking Dance Salon. For a
while the roof leaked and an entire cabinet of Guy Lombardo 78s were warped. But a tarpaulin and a bucket of
black tar did the trick. Mr Hawking concentrated on Junior
men, Youth dancers – men, of course, and Standard men
up to thirty-five. Mr Hawking developed a fine line in
French patter which didn't fail to impress. I used to listen
at the door. 'Sauté à coin then rond,' he'd shout. 'En avant
à coté then en dehors,' he'd call. 'Chaisé de dame then
jetté, chassé de l'homme then allemande.' It was so dig-
nified. But we couldn't understand why other dance
studios were booming and we were not. In fact we were
going downhill pas de zéphyr, with not a sauté pivot in sight.
Too late we discovered that most studios had merely become meeting places for young folk after the war to find
partners. Well, that was a refined way of putting it. I knew
what went on at Daphne and Vincent's Académie de
Danse on Dogkennel Hill. And you didn't require much
tuition for that. Mr Hawking just commenced a new
advertising campaign in *Dance News* magazine. This time
we tried to get single boys and girls to build their enthusiasm
for the art and craft. We had just started to engage a nice
clientele for the Youth comps when the blow fell. We had
just got back on our elevations when Modern Ballroom
tuition received its biggest blow since Denise and Frank
Sycamore drowned in the *Titanic* on their way to the World
Championships at Carnegie Hall. The blow, of course, was

rock'n'roll. We'd had storm warnings from across the Atlantic. First Guy Mitchell did some excruciating things to the quickstep. Then came Frankie Laine, and we all thought the tango would be simply swept away. Johnny Ray discs we could take, Pat Boone, Alma Cogan we could take, even Connie Francis – but rock'n'roll brought our dance salon to its knees. Closed dances were dropped. Even the introduction of the mambo novelty couldn't halt the slide. As for Daphne and Vincent's Académie de Danse on Dogkennel Hill, they went the way of all flesh. A Council health and hygiene officer closed it down on a Wednesday morning, nine o'clock sharp.

. . . In my time I had a classy jitterbug. I did Lindy Hop demonstrations to Italian POWs. Al Bowlly and Jack Plant. Who wanted those dances after the war was over? Mr Hawking could no longer afford to buy the latest Nat Gonella records for the salon. I was reduced to stitching rhinestones for young girls' appliqué bodices. I developed a new spray technique for turning chiffon into twinkle-chiffon. Girls couldn't afford to buy the new glitter-inlays being manufactured. There was an unfortunate complaint of some sort and Mr Hawking was ordered up to the Imperial Society's offices. He had an outright quarrel and resigned his accreditation as a qualified teacher. I didn't dare inquire further. I was too busy in my own mind. I knew what I wanted. For once in my life I got my own way. I wanted to adopt a little girl. And to my surprise and my delight – Mr Hawking jumped at the idea.

. . . She was four, and blonde with ringlets and a wire brace through her front teeth. She had lovely long legs and could already pirouette. She was called Kirsten. A lucky name in my book, I thought. Because ballroom dancing was becoming quite a rage in Scandinavia. Kirsten was the finest dance pupil we ever had. She came tenth in the Tiny Tots' Mecca awards at Sollihull. Mr Hawking and me put all our hopes in young Kirsten. How we loved her. She worked four hours a day on her routines. And never once complained. We knew she'd reach the stars. We entered her for

all the musical film auditions. We kept an eagle watch on
every television programme which required girl talent. We
took her one year to Butlins in North Wales for the Talent
Spot show, and the next month we took her all the way down
to Bristol to the Pontin's Holiday Special Talent contest.
It was gripping and nail-biting stuff. Kirsten stood up well
to it. She never cried once. She never showed her dis-
appointment. She fought back for us. Oh yes, and we once
had best stalls, and we pushed Kirsten up on the stage into
Frankie Vaughan's arms slap in the middle of his big
number.

. . . It was a Tuesday, first week in May, when the man
from the Foster Parents Office called. He said he did not
want to go into the details right now. But it was no longer
possible for us to keep Kirsten under our roof. He wouldn't
elaborate. And it was left to Mr Hawking to go back to the
head office. Mr Hawking stayed there all day. In the evening,
when he got back late, after I had tucked my little angel up
in bed, I knew from the look on his face. Some adoption
papers we had first signed had been rescrutinized. Mr
Hawking said the Foster Parents Office was now apprised
of the fact he spent two years in gaol during the war. We
were not acceptable parents. I collapsed on the lino in the
vestibule. I broke a strap on my shoe and crashed my
temple against the occasional-table. I lay in bed the day
they came to take her. I was numb and hollow. After she
kissed me good-bye, I heard her voice downstairs – she
cried out – 'Momma, don't let them! You are my momma!'
And the front door slammed.

. . . Mr Hawking and me still travel. We went to the Carl
Allen Awards in Dumfries in June, when His Imperial
Highness Prince Wikasa of Japan presented a special award
to the Nolan Sisters. Mr Hawking makes a point of asking
for twin beds at the hotel reception. He knows how I like
to sleep undisturbed. And he makes his little joke about our
'divan life'. When we work at local comp level we abide
by strict rules. We never speak. We never bump into each
other. We pretend we are not married. It helps keep the

impartial atmosphere of the comp. To him I am the Organizer and to me he is Mr Hawking. Of course, our private lives are quite different.

. . . I spend a lot of time trying to forget. He does, too. After Kirsten left, we did try a dance together. A sequence dance at an old fogeys' do. A Britannia Saunter I think. I tried to follow him. But I was at sea. I couldn't put a foot right, and all the time he wanted desperately to tell me, but he just couldn't bring himself to say it. Too much of a gent. I faulted each twinkle. I died on the floor. Those couples watching us. The shame. That was the last time we ever danced together. My hand in his glove. Since Kirsten was took away from us I've lost my step. And we both have learned to put things aside. I have my old wicker chair by the window where I lay out my clothes. He has his Pye Black Box in the front room where he plays his Creole love-call. His favourite. Mr Hawking understands. And he has always respected my wishes. Touch not the heart that already bleedeth.

[*Lights fade on the dressing-room.*
Out on the ballroom-floor area, TREVIS *and* AVRIL *continue their foxtrot. The* BAND *plays the quick-quick-slow rhythm. As our couple promenade before us –*]

TREVIS: . . . I want to know what the hell's going on, did you see what Artie just did?

AVRIL: . . . I've told you all I think you ought to know.

TREVIS: . . . Is there some conspiracy to ruin my chance at winning tonight a place in the top six? Is that it?

AVRIL: . . . It don't seem to concern you that Dot has a part in this.

TREVIS: . . . I'll bloody kill her.

AVRIL: . . . Whatever Dot did – you'd only reflect just what matters to you.

TREVIS: . . . So?

AVRIL: . . . You don't need Dot. What can she do for you? What good can she give by staying?

TREVIS: . . . I'll discuss Dot and me emotions any hour of the day but not in the middle of me bleeding foxtrot!

[*He does a Natural Hover Telemark (NHT) and heads for a feather finish somewhere away from us up-stage.*]

AVRIL: . . . She's going.

TREVIS: . . . It's a fit-up.

AVRIL: . . . You won't miss her.

TREVIS: . . . Right now, no!

[*They assume Line of Dance (LOD) and slow-quick-quick-slow away from us into the darkened ballroom area. Stars and spotlight fade. The* BAND *wraps up.*
To darkness.
Lights come up on the arcade curtain. DOT *and* ARTIE *stand ready, arms akimbo, toes on their mark, as the* BAND *strikes up a fine fanfare. Our couple close positions.*
Sudden darkness on the arcade curtain. The fanfare dies.
Lights on the dressing-room. AVRIL *and* TREVIS. GERRY *stands by the door.* AVRIL *looks oddly at* TREVIS. *He is trying to show her his nostrils.*]

TREVIS: Naah . . . go on, look.

AVRIL: I'd rather not.

TREVIS: Do the hairs show in me nostrils, that's all?

AVRIL: I haven't looked.

TREVIS: Course you have!

AVRIL: All right, they do!

[TREVIS *pulls out a pair of tiny curved clippers. He gives them to her. She sighs.*]

AVRIL: . . . Which nostril . . . ?

TREVIS: Both. You've always done both.

AVRIL: Trevis!

[*She shuts the clippers and hands them back to him.*]

GERRY: I'd noticed this young lad. He'd paid for a month's tuition at the salon. Green eyes, big feet and very thin hips. It just so happened you can't learn that rumba unless you've got oiled and generous hip talk. The hips have to talk. He stayed late after the other pupils had washed up. I said he had hips like cricket bats – No oil in them. I use a familiar technique with a pupil. I have to get behind them and grasp their buttocks in a firm hold. I have to mould their bums to the Ray McVay sway. The Scots have a great rumba tradition. I was determined to teach this lad right. And I had him in harness round and round the salon. Cucarachas-cucarachas-cuca-cuca-cuca-cucarachas and hockey-stick! Cucarachas-cucarachas and cuca-cuca-cuca-cu – and the record stopped. Perhaps I was a little long in removing my hands. I said, 'What's up?' And the boy burst into tears. Great retching sobs. He pulled himself together and muttered a quite insulting insinuation. And he asked for his tuition money back. I refused. He put his trees into his patents and stormed out. The next I knew I was hauled up in front of the Imperial Society. And I was stripped of my ISTD accreditation. Honest to God I cannot recall anything. I touched him. Perhaps he trembled. But that was all.

. . . As for Kirsten, our adopted little flaxen wonder, the chips were stacked. I must confess I never filled in the Foster Parents' form in detail. I wanted to, dear Lord. My pen was poised. I told myself that events which transpired in war-time get swept under a civilian carpet. What a fool. It took the Foster Authorities four years before they stumbled on the Warwick Internment camp. And my name. After that, it was all over save for the knock at the door. We did have four wonderful years with Kirsten. When they took her back I could not speak to my wife. I wanted to end it all for us. We tried to cheer ourselves up by joining the Society for Senior Dancers. A club affair really. You went there to grow old and to hide varicose veins with leg-tan. We did a Britannia Saunter in sequence. My wife stumbled on her first twinkle and she blushed magenta. There is no better time to tell your partner it is finished than when you are out there in the dark with the cruel spot. You cannot be more alone. More dependent on each other. More vulnerable. I wanted to say the marriage was through . . . say I'm sorry . . . I can see no end to us . . . We just career on madly. Oh yes, with etiquette. You curtsy. I acknowledge. Grip the hand with straight fingers. Keep toffee off white gloves. Ask but don't demand. Lead but don't run. Tits never to fall out of bra-cups. Try not to promenade with an erection before a member of the Greek Royal Family. Oh and that tale about the girl with no knickers who boogalooed at Chorlton-le-Fylde Hydro was grossly exaggerated. At the finale always escort your partner to her seat. There are rules you know. And Mum and dad died within a fortnight of each other in a month of frost. I never did say it in that Britannia Saunter. She was my shield. I picked up the threads of the salon. There was a bit of life yet in ballroom tuition. The disco dances have given us a new lease on the moment. At holiday venues, I encourage the fancy dress element. At various places along the North Wales coastline, I've organized a 'Dukes and Trollops Nite'. Then there was a 'Bishops and Bints' affair. 'Tycoons and Broads' I had. 'Majors and Crumpet' was a popular one. Oh and they dressed up they did. I had 'MPs and Slags', 'Dandies and Witches', 'Mutes and Shrews', 'Dons and Dragons' and I can see no end to us. How we career on madly ... towards ... quite unfinished ...

[*The dressing-room darkens. A spotlight picks up* ARTIE *and* DOT *as they step across the ballroom area in their foxtrot.*]

ARTIE: ... It's Trevis, init? Why didn't you have the gall to come out with it, first place?

DOT: ... It is not Trevis.

ARTIE: ... Who is he then?

DOT: ... She is not leaving with Trevis on the back of his bike, I promise you.

[*They enter a fast zigzag.*]

ARTIE: ... Just what's been going on behind my back? I want to know.

DOT: ... Crikey, Artie. Take care. This ain't a tango.

ARTIE: ... I don't care. I'll kill him. Whoever it is. I'll turn him into a right skiffle if I find out it's Trevis.

DOT: ... She told me to break it to you as gently as poss. She says it is finished. And she goes tonight.

ARTIE: ... I feel ill. I'm all in a twist.

[*They reach a back wall. She has to hold him firmly. He's wobbling.*]

DOT: ... I wish you would, mate!

ARTIE: ... Huh?

[*They abort. The Natural Twist Turn (NTT) is a cock-up. The* BAND *plays out the numbers.* ARTIE *totters and they try to finale together. Shaky.*
To darkness.
Lights in the dressing-room; ARTIE *and* DOT *come tearing back.* GERRY *has gone.*
ARTIE *marches up to* TREVIS. AVRIL *and* DOT *hang back.*]

ARTIE: ... 'Scuse I!

TREVIS: Oh yes?

ARTIE: I'm going to kill you!

TREVIS: Is that a threat?

[*Nose to nose.*]

ARTIE: What has happened to you, Trev, eh?

TREVIS: Well, actually, I'm lying in eighth position. I'm two points behind seventh. And I've a six-point advantage over that pair of Morris dancers in ninth.

ARTIE: For God's sake! Avril's leaving me!

TREVIS: Dot's leaving me, so what's new?

ARTIE: Eh?

TREVIS: Eh?

[TREVIS *picks* ARTIE *up by the chin.*]

... Dot's not going to live with you – is that the result of this contretemps? Have you acquired some new sexual techniques from the Rotary Club?

ARTIE: Put me down, Trev.

TREVIS: Where's Dot going?

ARTIE: Where's Av going?

AVRIL: Why don't you ask *us*?

DOT: Yearh, go on. Sit on the bench and let's talk for six hours without a break.

TREVIS: Shadap!

ARTIE [*to* DOT]: What does that mean?

[THE ORGANIZER *gives a clear banging on the door.*]

ORGANIZER'S VOICE: Couple number six! Thirty seconds! The tango please!

ARTIE: ... Dot ... Avril ... I want the truth.

AVRIL: But are you prepared to listen to the truth?

TREVIS: Oh no. Not before me tango, love.

ARTIE: Not me, mate. I'm having it right out now, right in the middle of the floor. If you want to play it rough – me too! OK?

[*He takes off his number '9' and turns it round to be number '6' on his coat.*]

TREVIS: What you doin', Art?

ARTIE: Avril's dancing with me.

TREVIS: She's not, she's my partner.

ARTIE: She's my wife and I'll set fire to your tails if you don't let me.

TREVIS: How can you?

ARTIE: Easy!

[*He swipes* TREVIS's *toupé off him and slaps it on his own bald patch.*]

... Nobody will notice the difference!

[ARTIE *snatches* AVRIL.]

TREVIS: You'll bugger me points. You can't dance with your wife! Hang on!

ARTIE: Too late!

[THE ORGANIZER *opens the door. She grabs* ARTIE *and* AVRIL *and shoves them out along the corridor.*]

ORGANIZER: Couple number six, move! Get tangoing, will you!

[TREVIS *stands at the door looking at them as they trot off.*]

TREVIS: You're joking. Don't leave me with Dot! Oi!

[*Lights fade in the dressing-room. Lights lift on the arcade curtain. The* BAND *strikes up a nice big intro for a tango.*

ARTIE *pulls himself together. Slaps his wig on tighter like a paratrooper about to take the big jump.* AVRIL *does her best. The tango surges.*]

ARTIE: ... Why?

AVRIL: ... I want my independence.

ARTIE: ... What for?

AVRIL: ... I cannot serve you any longer.

ARTIE: ... Explain it?

AVRIL: . . . I've had your kids. I've slept in your bed. I've run the home. Now I've had it.

ARTIE: . . . Why spring it in this fashion?

AVRIL: . . . There was no other way you'd take me seriously.

ARTIE: . . . Tradition and family life counts for nothing, I suppose?

AVRIL: . . . Family is an artificial concept designed to enslave women.

ARTIE: . . . What about love then?

AVRIL: . . . It is a universal means of emotional blackmail.

ARTIE: . . . What about the kids?

AVRIL: . . . You keep the kids.

ARTIE: . . . What about me?

AVRIL: . . . I've asked me mum to come down and look after you.

[*Into a Fall-away Promenade (FP).*]

ARTIE: . . . I can't breathe! It's my lungs! I'm in pain!

AVRIL: . . . Where? Oh, Art!

[*They dance on away from us into a darkened area as the spotlight fades and the* BAND *tempo fades away to nothing. Darkness. Just stars.*

Lights in the dressing-room. TREVIS *and* DOT. TREVIS *switches on the tannoy. Applause.*]

GERRY'S VOICE: . . . That was couple number six, Trevis and Avril. Jury says three 'twos', and three 'ones'. Now that's not your usual high standard, Trev dear. Where are all those lucky 'fours'? Keep your pecker cheerful, don't let the hard moments overtake you, and you'll be well out in front as the saying goes!

[TREVIS *peels back his lips and snarls at the tannoy. He blats it with his fist. It makes an unusual sound. And crackles out. He straightens his shirt.*

He grabs DOT, *and pulls her out of the door.*]

TREVIS: You!

DOT: Me?

[*She totters after him on her heels, her skirt billowing around her like a candyfloss cloud.*

Lights fade in the dressing-room.

Lights on the arcade curtain. As TREVIS *(with number '9' on his back) and* DOT *shape up for the* BAND's *fanfare, the spotlight hits them.*

Into their tango –]

TREVIS [*slow – walk – quick-quick-slow*]: . . . All right. Let's have it. What went wrong?

DOT: . . . One day last week I said to meself I cannot spend the rest of me life running away from you.

TREVIS: . . . You can rectify that by staying where you are.

DOT: . . . Then I said I just don't want to spend any more time in your bed.

TREVIS: . . . Oh, nice one.

DOT: . . . Because frankly it is the bed angle that gets me most.

TREVIS: . . . Oh so it's down to the angle of the old bed, is it? I haven't noticed.

DOT: . . . You haven't?

TREVIS: . . . It may squeak a bit.

DOT: . . . Trevis!

TREVIS: . . . You are referring to our love-making, I take it?

DOT: . . . I asked meself: do I want your children? The answer is no. Will I one day meet a guy I want to make love to night and day under the stars? The answer is – unlikely. On the other hand – do I want you?

TREVIS: . . . Get an answer, did you?

DOT: . . . I've run away from you, you've shrugged it off. I've insulted you, you've grown another skin. I'm sorry, Trev, it's over.

[*Into, perhaps, a progressive link and a Natural Twist Turn (NTT) but* TREVIS *makes a mistake.*]

. . . Watch it!

TREVIS: . . . Come back, Avril! Cobblers!

DOT: . . . Hold tight, Trev. It's all you've got left.

[*They dance on. The spotlight blinks off. The* BAND *fades.*]

TREVIS: . . . Gord! Me neck! Ow!

[*His shrill sudden cry. And darkness.*

Lights on in the dressing-room. ARTIE *sits straddle-wise over*

a chair clutching his chest. TREVIS *has cricked his neck in
such a way he can only look side-long.* AVRIL *and* DOT
beside them.]

ARTIE: . . . I've lost positive control of me breathing.

AVRIL: I'll do it.

ARTIE: Don't touch me. I won't have it.

AVRIL: I am the wife, arn'I?

ARTIE: I want my partner back.

AVRIL: Artie love –

ARTIE: I never want to dance with you again. You're too
quick around the pivots. Dot!

[DOT *holds his chest.*]

DOT: Just relax. Breathe nice and shallow.

ARTIE: I can feel it all going funny inside. I've had a stroke.

DOT: I'll ease the corselet. It's too tight.

[*She pulls up his shirt and loosens the corselet. She rubs his
chest and back with firm strokes.*

TREVIS *stands with his neck cocked at the one angle.*]

TREVIS: Oh yes? And what about me?

AVRIL: Trev – is there something wrong with your neck?

TREVIS: Wrong? What do you bollocking think I'm standing
like this for? To attract the judges!

AVRIL: Oh dear.

TREVIS: That bitch! She's done for me. Look at me!

DOT: He's cricked his neck, that's all.

TREVIS: Bitch!

DOT: That's right, what am I?

[AVRIL *gently helps* TREVIS *to lie flat on the bench.*]

AVRIL: Lie flat.

TREVIS: What do you know about necks?

AVRIL: Just enough to wring one.

DOT: Hallo, Trev, there. You'll look a daft bundle with your
face turned back to front in the paso doble.

TREVIS: You did this! Look at me!

AVRIL: Still! Please!

[*She gives* TREVIS'*s neck a hefty wrench to the other side.*]

TREVIS: Yeow!

[*He shakes his head. Sits up. It seems better.*]

DOT: There you go, Trev. It's no use looking like a right pain-in-the-neck in the last two dances, is it?

TREVIS: You can have no idea what you are doing to me. Weren't you satisfied with what we had? We had some laughs. I bought you that orange crash helmet. And don't give me any of that bed angle. I know what went on.

DOT: No you don't.

TREVIS: You know what I'm talking about. I never went to sleep without making sure you had those two things. Oh yes. You know all right. You know what I mean.

DOT: Things?

TREVIS: Don't play jejune with me.

DOT: Oh we're talking about orgasms, are we?

TREVIS: Kindly lower your voice.

DOT: Trev, they weren't orgasms. In recent months, they were just deep breaths.

TREVIS: Breaths? What about all that thrashing and heaving?

DOT: Go on!

TREVIS: What about that time you pulled the slat out of the Scandinavian bedhead?

DOT: It was for your benefit.

TREVIS: You mean to say when you bust that bedhead with your bare hands it wasn't an orgasm?

DOT: Yearh.

ARTIE: What's the next dance, Av?

AVRIL: Rock'n'roll.

TREVIS [to ARTIE and AVRIL]: Shadap!

ARTIE: I don't think orgasms is the fit subject for a dressing-room, Trev.

TREVIS: I do. I want it out. All out laid on the kitchen table right now, for all to see.

> [TREVIS and ARTIE collect their square-shouldered teddy-boy jackets from the hangers on the wall. They put them on. They also change shoes. They have thick-soled squelchies of a sort of art suede. The jackets are fingertip-drape. They take off their white bows, and dangle cowboy-style shoe laces on their shirtfronts.]

AVRIL: He's right, Artie. We've all got to have it out.

138

DOT [*to* TREVIS]: Well, you know how we make love. How we really do it. Nothing much happens, love. You don't really want me. You know it deep down, Trev. I do all the work. If people knew how much wrist action I put into our fore-play, I'd get an award for services to the piston principle.

TREVIS: We've come that low, eh? Right down into the steam-ing gutter? Oh you can put one over, Dot. I'm winded. You and I go back a long way on that bike. And those picnics on the South Downs. What about that time in the long grass and that broken strawberry yoghurt container? You got right under the belt. You hurt.

DOT: One day, you'll begin to tell me lies. That's when I don't want to be around. Future's short, Trev, but it's full of long nights.

TREVIS: Oh, artistic!

DOT: Yearh – if that's how you see it.

ARTIE: We shouldn't be overhearing this.

AVRIL: You take exception, do you?

DOT: It's the truth.

ARTIE: That what you call it?

> [*He is nervous and pulls his fingertip-drape straighter. He glances at the dance list on the back of the door.*]

. . . Rock'n'roll next, Trev.

TREVIS: Yearh . . . which one?

ARTIE: 'Sweet Little Sixteen.' Those were the days, eh?

AVRIL: No, they weren't.

> [ARTIE *and* AVRIL *look up.*]

ARTIE: That how you feel?

AVRIL: It is.

ARTIE: I'm beginning to hate you.

AVRIL: I don't want you to. But if that helps . . .

ARTIE: Slagging cow!

AVRIL: Yes.

ARTIE: Ace bitch, right?

AVRIL: OK.

> [ARTIE'*s hands open and close. He cannot decide. He turns to the tannoy and switches it on. Out on the dance floor the* BAND *is playing rock'n'roll for the first competitors.*

TREVIS *and* DOT *look at each other.*]

TREVIS: I'm going to dance your balls off!

DOT: It is not the lady who possesses them in the normal course of events.

TREVIS: Are you suggesting?

DOT: No.

TREVIS: I'll show you how to dance. I'll wet your knickers out there!

DOT: Up yours, Trev.

TREVIS: How dare you!

DOT: Right up!

TREVIS: Don't say things like that to me!

DOT [*little finger*]: Up!

[TREVIS *heaves inside his black drape – he looks like a cube of TNT on the boil. He crosses to the tannoy and raises the sound level of the music.*]

TREVIS [*elbowing* ARTIE *in a friendly but fierce manner*]: You wanna dance?

ARTIE: Eh?

TREVIS [*pulls* DOT *into the centre of the dressing-room*]: And you!

DOT: Trev – !

[ARTIE *pulls* AVRIL *into the middle of the room.* ARTIE *and* AVRIL *and* TREVIS *and* DOT *wade into the* r & r *number.*

It is as if once and only once these Chuck Berry warriors in a wattage of dream and anger will try to finish it together.

ARTIE *and* TREVIS *get the upper hand on the routines. But* DOT *and* AVRIL *give all they've got, too.*

TREVIS *behaves as if he would like to throw* DOT *against the wall. They rock through to the end of the number.*

From the tannoy we can hear the applause from the audience. ARTIE *switches the tannoy off.*

All four of them slump down. The girls sprawl across the seats, wiped out. The boys rest against the wall or on the floor, flaked. Glazed sweat and knackered fingertip-drapes.

THE ORGANIZER *knocks and pops her hear round the corner.*]

ORGANIZER: . . . Couples number six to ten, are you ready to rock'n'roll?

[*To darkness.*

We pause here. We can hear the BAND *tuning up again. Corridor* VOICES *and hum from the* CROWD.]

end of act two, scene one

ACT TWO

Scene Two

[*In the dressing-room all four,* ARTIE *and* TREVIS *and* AVRIL *and* DOT, *change into their Spanish gear. As a rule, the boys hold one-piece suits with bolero tops and extra high heels. The girls wear waisted dresses trimmed with a Latin flounce, and something spray-like in their hair.* TREVIS *is still without his toupé.* ARTIE *seems to want to hang on to it for support. It does not quite fit* ARTIE. *It has a droop in its crown, a certain hangdog effect.*

It isn't easy for TREVIS *to tuck his playboy underpants into his Spanish trousers.* ARTIE *cannot persuade the cat-suit to overcome his corselet.*

AVRIL *and* DOT *help each other with the zips on a bench. The boys struggle with their gear. Both girls are calm.*]

AVRIL [*to the boys*]: We have thought it out. Dot and me. And it is our decision – we are leaving together. We have grown very dependent on one another in the past. And we find we have shared all our problems and complaints. We like to be together. We enjoy sorting out each other. Mostly, we find we are very dependent on one another. We are proper partners in life. And that is that.

ARTIE: Together? With each other?

AVRIL: That is the rough translation, yes.

DOT: We have become very close.

TREVIS: Oh that's it! You're a couple of steaming left-handed five-shilling pound-note woofters!

AVRIL: We thought you'd say something like that, Trev.

DOT [*softly*]: It takes a woofter to find a woofter.

TREVIS: I take exception to that.

AVRIL: We are not lovers, Dot and me. We have discussed that issue. We came to the conclusion we are not and never shall be. We wish to stay together. Perhaps travel to foreign parts. Get jobs. Find a flat. We are friends. Real and true friends.

ARTIE: Why do this now?

DOT: Avril has been saying this to you for years, you've never listened.

AVRIL: As for Dot – how many more times must she run off for it to sink in?

TREVIS: I think now comes a time for some serious elbows on the table and let's get it all out hanging in the old breeze.

DOT: Talking is done with.

ARTIE: You mean you're not prepared to discuss this at all?

AVRIL: At all.

TREVIS: Eh?

[*Both girls shake their heads.*]

ARTIE: You sayin' you feel more for her than you do for the kids? Or the car? Have you considered properly the terms of our family insurance scheme?

AVRIL: I did love you once. Love has flown, Artie.

ARTIE: Oh, poetic!

AVRIL: I do not any more. As for the kids – do not blackmail me over them.

TREVIS [*to* DOT]: You've thievin' stole me number one dancing partner because you knew this was the one way to hurt. You right greasing bitch, Dorothy Dooly!

DOT: No, darling. Without me you'll be on yer tod. You won't have to rely on a woman. You'll be all right. You don't need me, Trev. Genuine.

ARTIE [*to* AVRIL]: I don't recall long talks about your greatest friend Dot. I don't believe Dot would ruin a promising career in local dance comps. No doctor's come to me with anything about the-end-of-your-tether pills. No woman has the right to just walk out on her family in this modern day and age. I didn't hear you say you never wanted to cook no more. I don't recall no row about the inability of the vacuum cleaner to achieve suction on the top-stair carpet. Who's going to stay in the house for when the bloke comes to repair the washing-machine? Who's going to tell him a white one about the maintenance contract being fully paid up? And who's going to talk to me mother-in-law when I'm in the garage? Mr Golding's annual shoe function at the Strand Palace?

Your new pair of winter boots every Christmas from the shop? I'm sorry but you've failed to convince me. I don't know what you two have got up to, but it's never going to happen.

[THE ORGANIZER *puts her head in the door.*]

ORGANIZER: Get your hats, boys, for the paso doble! Thirty seconds!

[*She goes out.*

DOT *takes two suitcases and places them just outside the door.*

AVRIL *takes the sombrero from the wall hook. Pops it on her head.*]

AVRIL [*to* ARTIE]: It isn't?

TREVIS: That's my Spanish flat hat, Avril.

DOT: Not tonight, Trev, not tonight.

[*Lights darken in the dressing-room.*

The BAND *fanfares the paso doble.*

Lights on the arcade curtains as AVRIL *and* DOT *stand on their points. Arms akimbo.*

The BAND *begins to crack up. The whole rhythm goes potty for a moment, as the girls parade.*

THE ORGANIZER *comes running from one direction. She is carrying all sorts of score-cards and official equipment.*

GERRY HAWKING *comes racing across the floor from another direction. In panic.*]

ORGANIZER: That's not couple number six!

GERRY: Stop them!

[THE ORGANIZER *and* GERRY HAWKING *collide and tumble together. They hang on to each other for dear life and roll across the floor in confusion. Arms and legs. They have never been so close.*

The BAND *picks itself up and crackles back into the correct tempo.*

AVRIL *and* DOT *alternate the bull and matador motif. They dance out the paso doble with vigour, under the white spotlight. Dancing for their lives.*

Catcalls. Whistles. THE ORGANIZER *and* GERRY *have picked themselves up. They help each other and hold tightly*

*to each other. They stand close together under a bright
spotlight. They commence to dust each other down.
Into darkness. Black silence.
Lights on a couple of golden chairs and a gilt table.* ARTIE
and TREVIS *walk over. They perch.*]

ARTIE: What I want to know is, what happened to the regulation boot with half a bottle of champagne-type bubbly for the booby prize?

[*Pause.*]

TREVIS [*tired*]: . . . I . . . was lying in eighth position . . . eighth.

ARTIE: Have you . . . ever asked yourself what's it all about?

TREVIS: Eh?

ARTIE: Have you ever come to the conclusion it's all about sticky fly-paper?

TREVIS: No, not really.

ARTIE: We go round and round the floor like flies, and always up ahead of you there's this great wad of sticky brown paper with a shine on it.

TREVIS: Oh, nasty.

ARTIE: . . . Have you . . . ever met my mother-in-law?

TREVIS: . . . You ever wanted something so bad you practically bleed for it . . . eh?

ARTIE: . . . Not really . . .

TREVIS: . . . No . . .

ARTIE: . . . Looking foolish I resist . . .

TREVIS: . . . It was going to be a surprise . . . but if I ever got through to the medals class . . . I was going to consider a dance studio meself for young executives . . . you know . . . for tired business types.

ARTIE: . . . Sure . . .

[ARTIE *takes off the toupé and gently hands it back to* TREVIS.]

ARTIE: . . . Sorry about that . . .

TREVIS: . . . Yearh . . .

[TREVIS *begins to crack. He leans forward to wipe the tears off. But they keep coming. Too many and too liquid they are.*]

ARTIE: . . . Think of the future . . .

TREVIS: ... Yearh ...

[TREVIS *cries like a baby. The tears run down amongst his chest hairs and his Muhammad Ali medallion.*]

ARTIE: ... S'all right ...

TREVIS: ... Oh yearh ...

ARTIE: ... S'all right ...

TREVIS: ... Yearh ... it's all right!

end

MORE ABOUT PENGUINS
AND PELICANS

For further information about books available from Penguins please write to Dept EP, Penguin Books Ltd, Harmondsworth, Middlesex UB7 0DA.

In the U.S.A.: For a complete list of books available from Penguins in the United States write to Dept CS, Penguin Books, 625 Madison Avenue, New York, New York 10022.

In Canada: For a complete list of books available from Penguins in Canada write to Penguin Books Canada Ltd, 2801 John Street, Markham, Ontario L3R 1B4.

In Australia: For a complete list of books available from Penguins in Australia write to the Marketing Department, Penguin Books Australia Ltd, P.O. Box 257, Ringwood, Victoria 3134.

MICHAEL HASTINGS

Three Plays

Gloo Joo

Winner of the Evening Standard Best Comedy Award

'Michael Hastings has produced two giant dramatic creations: the unspeakable Idi Amin in *For the West* (*Uganda*), and now in *Gloo Joo* a satisfying comic counterpart – Meadowlark Rachel Warner. Man, did it satisfy ma soul!' – *Time Out*

Full Frontal

'Full of measured innocence, sarcasm and spleen – funny and moving' – *Gay News*

For the West (Uganda)

'Tough, gripping, puzzling ... I have a sneaking suspicion that it's a great play' – *Punch*

ARTHUR MILLER

Death of a Salesman

Death of a Salesman was written in six weeks in the spring of 1948, but it had been brewing in Miller's mind for ten years. Its 742 performances put it among the 50 longest recorded Broadway runs; it received the Pulitzer Prize for Theatre and was later filmed. Miller himself defined his aim in the play as being 'to set forth what happens when a man does not have a grip on the forces of life'.

A View from the Bridge / All My Sons

A View from the Bridge, which was filmed in 1962, deals with the problem of illegal immigration into America. The presence of two Italian immigrants brings to the surface the hidden tensions within an American family, and leads to eventual tragedy. *All My Sons* won the American Critics' award in 1947. In it Arthur Miller examines a businessman's responsibility for a wartime disaster by confronting the different scales of values of father and son.

and

After the Fall
The Crucible
The Price

Fiction from dramatists in Penguins

SAMUEL BECKETT

The Expelled and Other Novellas

'I'm working with impotence, ignorance,' Beckett once wrote. These four stories, *First Love*, *The Expelled*, *The Calmative* and *The End*, were written soon after the Second World War and are characterized by his concern with the helpless individual consciousness. As well they are rich in verbal and situational humour and offer a fascinating insight into the work of a writer who has transformed both the art of the novel and contemporary theatre.

ARNOLD WESKER

Love Letters on Blue Paper and other stories

'Integrity and a deep sense of pity are the qualities that emerge from these thoughtful stories' – *Sunday Times*

ARTHUR MILLER

Focus

'I have tried to confront a man with his own hallucination', wrote Miller when *Focus* was first published in 1945. The hallucination is racial prejudice against the Jews, and this book is as chilling and important now as it ever was.

BERNARD SHAW

Cashel Byron's Profession

Bernard Shaw was obsessed with prize-fighting all his life – he entered the English Amateur Boxing Association Championship as a middleweight – and his racy, romantic adventure story superbly evokes the bruised knuckles and raw hopes of the ringside. 'Genuine and remarkable narrative talent . . . a talent of strength, spirit, capacity . . . It is all mad, mad and deliriously delightful . . . All I ask is more of it' – Robert Louis Stevenson